VIRGINIA O'HARE REVEALS

GOD'S FINAL JUDGMENT ON HUMANITY

PRAISE FOR VIRGINIA O'HARE

"Virginia O'Hare has done it again! Her newest book [Virginia O'Hare Reveals God's Final Judgment on Humanity], tells the frightening truth of God's Word for anyone on the planet that does not know our Lord and Savior, Jesus Christ, as their only pathway to an eternity in Heaven. We see the events that are unfolding all around us with increasing speed. From a global pandemic to Russia's invasion of Ukraine, the End-Times signs are very visible to those who know what to see. As God's choice to wear the Mantle of the Last-Day Prophet, Virginia fulfills that charge to warn everyone around the world of the soon-coming events and the consequences of ignoring God's truth."

"What an incredible and inspiring book, [Virginia O'Hare's Trials, Triumphs, and Vision from God]. It was so gripping that I could not put it down once I started reading it. Each page made me want to learn more about what happened next in Virginia's life. Most people would have given up and decided that they were handed a bad lot in life. But not Virginia. She was driven by God and determined to move forward despite the many tragedies and difficult situations she faced in her life. I was so inspired that I read it twice. I recommend it to anyone wishing to strengthen their faith or searching for their faith."

"Virginia is a skilled writer who elegantly tells a captivating tale of her son's fascinating story and her unbelievable relationship with God, inspiring her and allowing her to write so beautifully. This book [Virginia O'Hare Documents God's Law Vs. Man's Law] is for those interested in the criminal justice system or furthering their relationship with God."

"Virginia truly has a gift of seeing visions from God. She has been through more than most people have been through and has the ability to stay positive and have such an upbeat, inspiring attitude. She has been such a blessing to my family through friendship and her spirituality and guidance. She has a true gift, and I highly recommend reading her books. They will change your life. They have changed mine and my wife's and have been such a blessing for our family."

"I am not typically one to leave a review, but in this case, [Virginia O'Hare Documents God's Law Vs. Man's Law], I felt it was important as it profoundly impacted my life. I thoroughly enjoyed the battle between what's right and what's wrong, and the insightful view on both sides opened my eyes to my own life. This is truly a book everyone should read."

"An inspiring story filled with trials and triumphs. [Virginia O'Hare's Trials, Triumphs, and Vision from God] Any person facing surgery trials and family difficulties will learn much about how they can respond with faith and hope."

"Virginia O'Hare's writing style has made her an international Best Seller! She does not ever 'sugar-coat' the truth. Her newest book warns the world of God's final judgment on humanity, and it is not a pretty picture for those who have not accepted Jesus Christ as their personal Savior. This book should not only scare the H*** out of you, but it should also scare YOU out of your direct pathway to HELL!"

DEDICATION

This book is dedicated to God Almighty, His Son Jesus Christ, the Holy Spirit, my three children, now in heaven, Anne Marie, Patricia Lynne, Robert Anthony; and 100,000,000 souls saved by God, through this author, a servant of the Lord.

TABLE OF CONTENTS

Preface　I
God's Calling on Virginia O'Hare's
Life 43 Years Ago

Introduction　IX
Virginia O'Hare's Spiritual
Communion with God

Chapter One　1
World War III is on the Horizon
—Who Will Win?

Chapter Two　9
God's Final Twenty-One
End-of-Days Judgments

Chapter Three　25
End-of-Days Events are
Now Converging

Chapter Four　33
Current Prophetic Signs of Upheavals
in the U.S. and Globally

Chapter Five　43
Only God Knows the Day and
Hour of Jesus' Second Coming!

Chapter Six　51
The Battle of Armageddon

Chapter Seven　59
What Happens to Believers at
Jesus' Second Coming?

Chapter Eight　63
What Happens After
the Battle of Armageddon?

Chapter Nine
Jesus Christ Judges Both
Believers and Non-Believers ... 67

Chapter Ten
The Holy Trinity: God, Jesus,
and the Holy Spirit ... 81

Chapter Eleven
Old Testament Prophets'
Accounts of the Jewish Messiah ... 89

Chapter Twelve
The Crucifixion of Jesus Christ ... 99

Chapter Thirteen
The Holy Spirit Dwells Within
Every Believer Eternally ... 105

Chapter Fourteen
Lucifer Cast Out of Heaven
Down to Earth ... 111

Chapter Fifteen
God's Final Warning to
This Generation ... 127

Chapter Sixteen
U. S. Declaration of Independence,
Constitution, & Bill of Rights ... 133

Chapter Seventeen
Three Lake County Sheriff
Deputies Brutally Beat My Son ... 143

My Life in Pictures ... 185

PREFACE

God's Calling on
Virginia O'Hare's Life
43 Years Ago

One evening, 43 years ago, while I was standing on a bridge, next to my point lot waterfront residence in Ft. Lauderdale, FL, where I lived with my husband and three grown children, I had a miraculous visitation from God. The moon and stars were sparkling on the waterway. No one was driving by. The only sound was an indescribable voice coming from the sky calling my name, "Virginia!" I looked up and saw the face of a man surrounded by clouds. As he talked to me, I saw His mouth open and close and heard this most astounding voice speaking to me. I felt peace and love come over me. His voice was thunderous and resounding like a combination of several waterfalls and earthquakes blending together. His words were audible, distinct, and clear. He said, "Virginia, in you, I am well pleased. I have chosen you to be my last-day prophet, and through you, ten million souls will be saved."

My first thought was, "only ten million souls?" He knew what I was thinking and said, "Ten times ten million souls will be saved through you." Then my mind questioned, without having any fear or trepidations, "am I really seeing and hearing God?" I had read in the Bible that no one can see God face to face and live. Yet I was still alive!!! Then I looked away from the vision and thought again, "Am I really seeing and hearing God? Knowing my thoughts, He answered, "So you know this is from Me, your picture will be on the front page of the newspaper, and everyone in the world will know who you are."

Following the visitation, I hurried, excitedly, into my home and shared this visitation from God with my family. My 20-year-old son, Robert Anthony, said, "Mom, don't tell anyone you saw God; they'll think you're crazy." When my son passed away at the age of fifty-eight, he said, "Mom, you need to fulfill what God called you to do and save souls for Jesus so that they won't burn in hell."

Shortly thereafter, my picture was on the front page of the Sun-Sentinel in Ft. Lauderdale, FL., and news reporters from around the world were calling my office, clamoring to interview me. This was because I had just won a large award in New York Supreme Court against a world-renowned plastic surgeon for medical malpractice. News reporters from other countries were flying into Poughkeepsie, New York to interview me at my Employment Agency in Poughkeepsie, New York, where I had been licensed by the State of New York for 9 years. The phone was ringing off the hook non-stop for days from reporters worldwide.

This notoriety caused me to sell my 9-year-old very successful Employment Agency and move to Ft. Lauderdale, Florida, where I remain today.

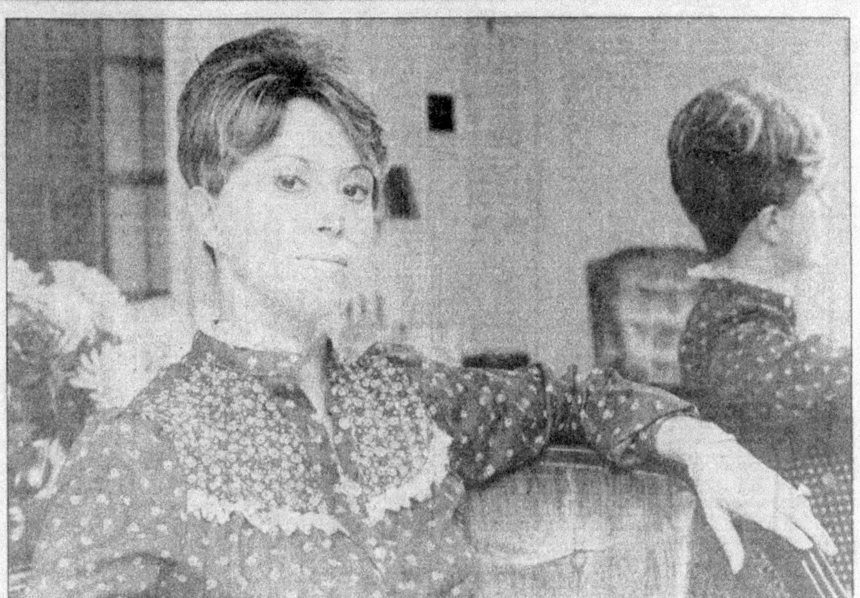

Fort Lauderdale News

Lifestyle

Wednesday, July 7, 1982

Staff photo by DEBORAH MEEKS

Virginia O'Hare has been living in Fort Lauderdale since her famed 1979 malpractice suit over a tummy-tuck operation.

Virginia O'Hare

A botched bellybutton leads to a book for the Lord

By Nora Frenkiel
Staff Writer

"In January of 1979, I received a vision of a large TV screen in which I was on the screen and there were newspapers flashing in front of me from all over the country and my picture was on the front page."

Virginia O'Hare is speaking with a strange mixture of detachment and child's wonder. While listening to her, you focus on her eyes — eyes that seem to blink of their own accord.

You focus on the surroundings: the Northeast Fort Lauderdale canal-side home with plastic covers on the dining room chairs, the home that is as immaculately kept as the woman herself. The 45-year-old face is unmarred by wrinkles. She is slender and petite, and favors pastel blouses and slim skirts.

It has been three years since Miss O'Hare's vision came true.

In May 1979, she became an instant celebrity after a jury awarded her $854,219 in a malpractice suit against Dr. Howard Bellin, a prominent New York plastic surgeon. Ms. O'Hare claimed Bellin misplaced her bellybutton during a tummy-tuck operation in 1974.

"I could go into a subway in New York and I could see my picture on the cover of the *Post*. It was a real strange feeling. What I wanted to do, since I was from a small town (Poughkeepsie, N.Y.), was scream. They got my picture.' "

She was a willing co-conspirator in the exploitation, the sensationalism that splashed her face and body across front pages and made her the curiosity of the week in *People* magazine. She talked willingly to anyone who asked about "the horror."

More than eight years have passed since her surgery and Ms. O'Hare, who was viewed as both victim and opportunist, finally fled the spotlight for seclusion and anonymity in Fort Lauderdale after the verdict. Yet she seems anxious to thrust herself back into its cruel glare.

Why would she subject herself to exposure again? Her answers go roundabout and settle at the beginning, the botched surgery.

"I feel very strongly that an injustice was done to my body," she says in a cool, detached voice. "What I went through when they did the unveiling was the worst moment of my life."

She sees herself as a symbol for all victims.

"I got very upset when I see people being taken advantage of, exploited, hurt, maliciously persecuted."

She leads you to the den, where there is a small bookcase crammed with medical textbooks on plastic surgery and

> I am writing a book that is divinely directed to give people a true picture of what it's like to undergo this trauma, this horrendous experience. I know it will be beneficial to people.

scrapbooks of the publicity surrounding her case.

She displays the gruesome Instamatic shots that recorded "the worst moment of my life."

"Look at this," she says of a particularly ugly snapshot of an abdomen scarred and bruised, and your hands reach out to touch what your eyes do not wish to see.

The issue of surgery remains an open wound. "I was butchered and the most important award I got was knowing I got justice in the courts. It wasn't something you get over, because somebody gives you a few thousand dollars. The money, quite honestly, was mostly given up by me.

Because the surgeon's insurance company was bankrupt, the case went to New York State's insurance commissioner who reached an agreement with Ms. O'Hare. She settled for $200,000 and moved her family to Fort Lauderdale.

"The Lord directed me here," she says.

Please see O'HARE, 5D

Virginia O'Hare

BELLY BUTTON APPEAL: A plastic surgeon says he will appeal a jury award to a woman whose belly misplaced. "She beat the system," Dr. Howard Bellin. "But I'll appeal. It was the most absurd amount of money. For a belly button! People who lose arms and legs only get $300,000." However, the owner of the off-center umbilicus, 42-year-old Virginia O'Hare, said: "A centered belly button is a valuable feminine attribute. (Singer) Cher made millions on hers." Mrs. O'Hare underwent a 1974 operation for a "tummy tuck" after Bellin promised her "a nice flat belly." Instead she emerged from the anesthetic to find her navel was off center. "The belly button, no longer normal, was a large deformed hole and the scar was of significant thickness," her attorney, Theodore Friedman, told a state Supreme Court jury of four men and two women. In her complaint, Mrs. O'Hare said her sex life suffered and her sense of "self worth" was damaged because of the non-centered navel. She also claimed her ability to function as owner of a Poughkeepsie employment agency was impaired. The position of her navel has since been corrected by another doctor.

Surgeon must pay: He's off the button

NEW YORK (UPI) — A misplaced belly button has cost a well-known New York City plastic surgeon $850,000 in damages.

Virginia O'Hare, 42, of Poughkeepsie, N.Y., and Fort Lauderdale, Fla., won the money yesterday from Dr. Howard Bellin. She said he botched her tummy-tightening surgery nearly three years ago.

O'Hare said she was grateful to the state Supreme Court jury of four men and two women for its "fair" decision in her $3 million suit.

She said Bellin had promised to give her a "nice, flat sexy belly," but instead she wound up with unsightly scars and a belly button two inches off center.

Her lawyer, Theodore Friedman, said the operation cut O'Hare "in half physically and emotionally." She testified that her business and sex life suffered as a result.

The jury, which heard the two-week-long trial in Manhattan, deliberated four hours before returning its verdict.

...months of anguish I had to endure make me ...O'Hare said.

...pain and suffering...and...an employ... Bellin, who is married... rebuilt O'Hare's nose and eyelids before...

Virginia O'Hare

VIRGINIA O'HARE
... awarded $854,219

Doctor Says He'll Appeal Navel Award

NEW YORK (AP) — A plastic surgeon says he will appeal a jury's $854,219 award to a woman whose belly button he misplaced.

"She beat the system," declared Dr. Howard Bellin. "But I'll appeal. It was the most absurd amount of money. For a belly button! People ...arms and legs only get ... owner of the off..., 42-year-old Vir...d: "A centered belly... valuable feminine attribute. ...er) Cher made millions on hers."

Mrs. O'Hare underwent a 1974 operation for a "tummy tuck" after Bellin promised her "a nice flat belly." Instead, she says she emerged from the anesthetic to find that her navel was off center by two inches.

"The belly button, no longer normal, was a large deformed hole in her stomach and the scar was of significant thickness," her attorney, Theodore Friedman, told a state Supreme Court jury of four men and two women.

In her complaint, Mrs. O'Hare said her sex life suffered and her sense of "self worth" was damaged because of the non-centered navel. She also claimed her ability to function as owner of a Poughkeepsie employment agency was impaired.

The position of her navel has since been corrected by another doctor.

Misplaced belly button costs doctor $854,000

(c) 1978 N.Y. Times News Service

NEW YORK — A ... old Poughkeepsie, N.... an $854,000 ...

...off center; Dr. ...was only half an inch off. ...he called "not cosmetically unacceptable."

Dr. Bellin called Wednesday's verdict "ludicrous" and expressed confidence it would be overturned on appeal. "People who lose arms and legs in automobile accidents don't get that kind of money," the surgeon said.

He added that the stomach operation he had performed on Mrs. O'Hare fol...

...he did on her nose and eyelids. "She told me she was going to double my practice," Dr. Bellin said.

The doctor, who is 43 years old, said he had been a plastic surgeon for 10 years and was now chief of plastic surgery at the Cabrini Health Care Center in lower Manhattan. "I've performed operations on 3,000 patients, and this is the first time anyone has collected a nickel from me," he said.

Mrs. O'Hare's lawyer, Theodore Friedman, told the jury that Dr. Bellin's operation had left "a large deformed hole" in his client's stomach.

Her belly button was moved back to its proper place in an operation performed by Dr. Philip Casson one year after Dr. Bellin's operation. Dr. Casson testified on behalf of Mrs. O'Hare at the two-week trial before Justice Alvin Klein in State Supreme Court. The jury deliberated four hours before rendering its verdict.

Hosp chief makes waves with belly-flop testimony

By D.J. SAUNDERS

The chief of plastic surgery at New York Hospital-Cornell Medical Center testified yesterday that he believes Virginia O'Hare was "betrayed" by the doctor who gave her an off-center bellybutton.

Dr. Dicran Goulian told a Manhattan Supreme Court jury that the New York State Medical Malpractice Panel, of which he was a member, unanimously voted last year to recommend the assessment of liability against O'Hare's physician, the socialite plastic surgeon Dr. Howard Bellin.

O'Hare, 42, says Bellin talked her into having "a belly-lift"—an operation that would give her "a nice, flat, sexy belly."

Wants 1.5 M

Instead, she says, she wound up with a big, ugly scar, a damaged psyche and a navel that was two inches off-center. She is suing Bellin for $1.5 million.

Goulian was the medical member of the malpractice panel—it also has a Supreme Court justice member and an attorney member—when O'Hare's case came up for review. He said the complained-of result was "most offensive" and added that "an off-center navel is very rarely encountered."

O'Hare contends that Bellin promised she would have only a "hairline scar" after the surgery. Goulian said he believes Bellin fostered "unreasonable expectations ... it is never possible to get a hairline scar after this surgery ... I felt this patient had been betrayed by her physician."

O'Hare, who lives in Fort Lauderdale, Fla., testified in a whimper that before the surgery her "tummy" ... "was in good condition ... it was not a distasteful, ugly stomach."

Describes the pain

O'Hare later broke down in uncontrollable sobs, causing Justice Alvin Klein to call a recess after she described the "excruciating" pain that she felt for five days after the operation, when Bellin allegedly did not visit her at the hospital.

"Blood was dripping down my leg," she said. "I saw this opening ... It's like I saw this cut ... it was just ghastly. I was in pain and I was ableeding...My doctor wasn't there.

"I saw this hole (her bellybutton) on the left side of my stomach," she said. "I was very upset that my body had been invaded and cut up for no reason."

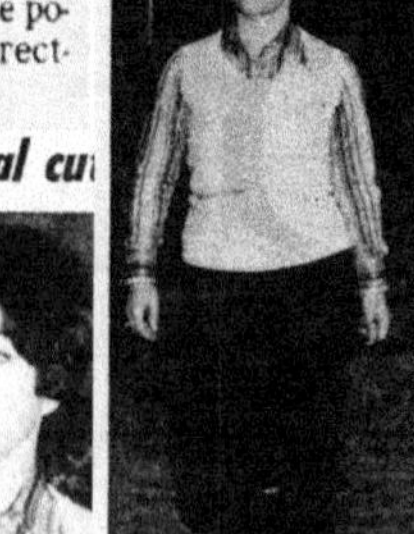

News photo by Michael Lipack
Virginia O'Hare at Supreme Court where she is suing for $1.5 million.

45G for abominable abdominal cut

By STEWART AIN and DONALD SINGLETON

A Manhattan Supreme Court awarded $854,219 yesterday Virginia O'Hare, the 42-year-old woman who came out of abdominal plastic surgery with an off-center belly-button.

Mrs. O'Hare's navel was moved two inches from its original location...the award comes to $127,105 per...

Yesterday's verdict followed an day trial of O'Hare's medical malpractice suit against the well-known surgeon Dr. Howard Bellin, who in '74 reportedly offered to give her a flat belly.

Sued for pain

Its award, the jury of four men and two women ruled that O'Hare was entitled to $600,000 for "pain and suffering" resulting from the botched tummy-tightening operation. The award included $4,219 in medical costs and $250,000 for "loss of earn..."

She first went to Bellin in 1973 for a nose job. The operation was such a success that she also had him fix up her eyelids.

But the abdominal plastic surgery that Bellin performed the following year, O'Hare said, was a disaster. She said she woke up after the operation in "extensive pain" and saw that there were "gaps in the incision ... with fat oozing out."

"Her umbilicus was off-center," said O'Hare's lawyer, Theodore Friedman. "The belly button, no longer normal, was a large deformed hole in her stomach and the scar was of significant thickness."

Some of the most damaging testimony at the trial came from Dr. Dicran Goulian, the chief of plastic surgery at New York Hospital-Cornell Medical Center, who told the court he believed that O'Hare had been "betrayed" by her surgeon.

Goulian said the New York State Medical Malpractice Panel, of which he was a member, last year unanimously voted to recommend the assessment of liability against Bellin.

Bellin, a socially prominent plastic...

Virginia O'Hare
Awarded $854,219

Accidents will happen

A SALESMAN in his early 40s thought it would do wonders for his business if he had the bags under his eyes removed. He went into surgery and got rid of the bags, but he came out with one eye smaller and lower than the other and with diminished vision in one eye.

An attractive 65-year-old widow wanted a new face. During the facelift operation the surgeon cut a nerve. Now her right shoulder droops and she's unable to use her right arm. She looks older than she did before the operation.

A 44-year-old physician's wife had a breast reconstructed following a mastectomy. The new breast was not the same size as her other breast and the nipple ended up in the vicinity of her armpit.

A 20-year-old college girl with pendulous breasts felt she would be much happier not being so top heavy. She decided to have her breasts surgically reduced. After the operation she was horribly scarred, her breasts were each a different size and the nipples were out of line. She broke up with her boyfriend, would accept no dates with other men and became more and more reclusive.

All of these people went into surgery with dreams of looking younger or better. Instead, they got nightmares for results, and ended up suing their surgeons for malpractice.

Botched cosmetic surgery cases became big news three weeks ago, when a Manhattan jury awarded more than $850,000 to Virginia O'Hare, whose bellybutton was moved off-center by Dr. Howard Bellin.

Sagging facelifts, eyes that won't close, ugly scars, bulging noses, mismatched breasts, cut nerves — these are all things that can go wrong when you go under the knife for cosmetic reasons.

Possible? Yes. Likely? No. Reputable surgeons say the chances of anything serious going wrong with plastic surgery are about 1%, and even then most mistakes can be corrected with a second operation.

"Plastic surgery is subject to the complications of any operation — bleeding, infections, disruptions of the wound. Any surgery exposes a patient to risk," said Dr. Laurence LeWinn, assistant professor of plastic surgery at the New York Hospital Cornell Medical Center. "But the majority of people have the statistics in their favor and will sail right through without problems."

"Any time you cut the human skin with a knife, there is some chance of complication," said Dr. John Goin, chairman of the public education committee for The American Society of Plastic and Reconstructive Surgeons. "It is clearly much more important to inform someone about the complications of a facelift than of a cance[r] ... in because the lift is optional."

Botched cosmetic surgery can produce ugly scars, bulging noses, cut nerves

[...] look like you're 20, I don't think you should go to that doctor.

"But if you go to a qualified doctor and a good hospital, the chances are very slim that you will have any major complication."

Reputable plastic surgeons contend that most mistake are made by [...] practitioners or by doctors in [...] attempting to perform [...] Patients can avo[...] they say, [...] they choose [...]

EVEN THEN, success is not necessarily assured. Virginia O'Hare, the famous bellybutton patient, had been to Howard Bellin for earlier operations on her nose and eyelids; she went [...] to him a third time because she was [...] with the work he had done.

[...] entails different risks [...] take those pos[...] [...]elift, the [...] ording [...] e. "The [...] ss than [...] y be re-

[...] Some [...] develop hematoma — [...] ood under the skin. These [...] ctions are usually small and dissolve [...] themselves in a few days. In a small percentage [of] cases, secondary surgery is necessary [to] remove them.

Probably about 10% of p[...] have eyelid operations [...] tion for a while [...] "It's not per[...] while [...]

[...] pletely. [...] to re-operate [...] skin but the chances [...] ng in experienced hands is [...] an one per cent," LeWinn said.

"Complications with the nose are less disabling than the other things we've talked about," said LeWinn. "One of the most common complications is a bulge just above the tip of the nose called a parrot's beak. There is probably not a plastic surgeon alive, no matter how competent, who has not had the disappointment of a patient with a parrot's beak. Fortunately it can be corrected with a second operation."

Breast surgery presents other problems. In breast augmentation, says Dr. Goin, the main risk is development of some firmness in the breast. "This can occur in 20% to 30% of cases and can vary from slightly firmer than normal to unacceptably firm." In breast reduction, he says "the scars are more extensive that most people imagine they will be and there is a substantial risk of loss of sensation in the nipples."

In reconst[...] of breasts after mastectom[...] d, results vary from [...] lent. Some recon[...] others do not. But [...] quite acceptable [...] ptable in clothing [...] t. It's rare to find [...] ed with reconstruction [...] ust the joy of not having to [...] r a prosthesis is so great.

"The point is that even if complications occur," LeWinn added, "we should be able to correct them. But it's important that patients expect a realistic result and don't expect to look like they're 20 again."
—B.S.

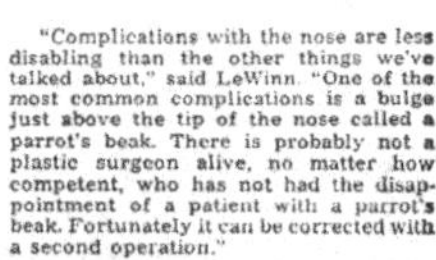
It cost Dr. Howard Bellin $854,000 when he misplaced...

...Virginia O'Hare's bellybutton. It was O'Hare's third operation.

Virginia O'Hare smiles after winning $854,219 in court yesterday.

Navel battle nets her 854G

By STEWART AIN and DONALD SINGLETON

A Manhattan Supreme Court jury awarded $854,219 yesterday to Virginia O'Hare, the 42-year-old woman who came out of abdominal plastic surgery with an off-center bellybutton.

Since O'Hare's navel was moved about two inches from its original location, the award comes to $427,109 per inch.

Yesterday's verdict followed an eight-day trial of O'Hare's medical malpractice suit against the well-known plastic surgeon, Dr. Howard Bellin, who in 1974 reportedly offered to give her "a nice, flat belly."

Awarded 100G for pain

In its award, the jury of four men and two women ruled that O'Hare was entitled to $100,000 for "pain and suffering" resulting from the botched [...]

Tummy-tightening operation botched

VIRGINIA O'HARE

NEW YORK (UPI) — A misplaced bellybutton has cost a well-known New York City plastic surgeon $850,000 in damages.

Virginia O'Hare, 42, Poughkeepsie, N.Y., and Fort Lauderdale, Fla., won the money Wednesday from Dr. Howard Bellin, a socially prominent plastic surgeon she claimed botched her tummy-tightening surgery nearly three years ago.

Mrs. O'Hare said she was grateful to the state Supreme Court jury of four men and two women for its "fair" decision in her $3 million suit.

Dr. Bellin, she said, had promised to give her a "nice, flat sexy belly," but instead, she wound up with unsightly scars and a bellybutton two inches off center.

Her attorney, Theodore Friedman, said the operation cut Mrs. O'Hare "in half physically and emotionally." She testified that her business and sex life suffered as a result.

The jury, which heard the two-week-long trial in Manhattan, deliberated four hours before returning its verdict.

"All the months of anguish I had to endure make me realize there is justice," Mrs. O'Hare, who is divorced, said.

The jury awarded her $100,000 for pain and suffering, $4,219 for medical expenses for corrective surgery and $750,000 for loss of earnings. Before the operation, she owned an employment office in Poughkeepsie.

Bellin, who is married to Countess Christina Paolozzi, had rebuilt Mrs. O'Hare's nose and eyelids before performing the stomach operation.

Today, my quest, as an internationally best-selling Christian author, is to use my four God-inspired books, as a vehicle to spread the Gospel of Jesus Christ; seek justice for my deceased son, Robert Anthony, and others, and proclaim God's 10 Commandments worldwide. God gave every human being free will with the inalienable right of life, liberty, and the pursuit of happiness. The United States Declaration of Independence confirms these rights and that they were given to us by our creator. Our governments are created to protect those rights for every American citizen, regardless of race, color, religion, or creed!!!

On June 11, 1776, President Thomas Jefferson included these God-given rights of life, liberty, and the pursuit of happiness, when he drafted the Declaration of Independence. He wanted a government that would safeguard those three God-given rights for every American citizen in our country and for throughout all time. My quest is to fulfill God's calling on my life, and be a vessel for Him to bring 100,000,000 souls into His Kingdom through repentance and faith in His Son Jesus Christ and to proclaim our God-given rights for everyone worldwide.

King Solomon wrote in 935 B.C. the following: "There is nothing better for a man than that he should eat and drink, and that he should make his soul enjoy good in his labour" (Ecclesiastes 2:24 KJV). "Fear God and keep His commandments: for this is the whole duty of man" (Ecclesiastes 12:13 KJV). "He has made everything beautiful in its time. He has also set eternity in the human heart, yet no one can fathom what God has done from beginning to end. I know that there is nothing better for people than to be happy and to do good while they live. That each of them may eat and drink, and find satisfaction in all their toil—this is the gift of God. I know that everything God does will endure forever; nothing can be added to it and nothing taken from it. God does it so that people will fear him. Whatever is has already been, and what will be has been before, and God will call the past to account. And I saw something else under the sun: In the place of judgment—wickedness was there, in the place of justice—wickedness was there. I said to myself, 'God will bring into judgment both the righteous and the wicked, for there will be a time for every activity, a time to judge every deed'" (Ecclesiastes 3:11-17 NIV).

This book declares God's love, His commandments, and warning to the entire human race that we are the final generation who will see the Second Coming of Jesus Christ. I pray for everyone reading this God-inspired book that all will accept Jesus Christ as their Lord and Savior, be filled with the Holy Spirit, and be ready for the soon coming of our Lord and Savior, who will bring every believer home to the Kingdom of God for all eternity!

INTRODUCTION

Virginia O'Hare's
Spiritual Communion with God

I, Virginia O'Hare, came boldly to God's throne, in the third heaven, which is filled with majesty, love, mercy, grace, and prayed for wisdom and knowledge of God's life before and after creating the universe and mankind. I wanted to share this awesome revelation in my fourth published book and give the honor and glory to the one and only true God of the universe, Jehovah, who I've loved and known for 85 years of my life.

As a child growing up in a large Italian family, I knew instinctively right from wrong and knew I had a special insight into life. I didn't realize exactly how to use it until I became a mature Christian by earnestly seeking, praying, and studying the Word of God. I had visions and spiritual writings given to me since childhood. I was born with a veil over my face and was told this was why I had a supernatural ability to perceive future events beyond normal sensory perception.

Later in life, when I was 42 years old, God honored me with an audible and visual visitation, which I detail in my first published book, *Virginia O'Hare's Trials, Triumphs, and Vision from God. **Barnes & Noble advertised this book as the BEST BOOK TO READ FOR 2020.***

God granted me the desire of my heart to know more about Him and His life before creation. I heard in my spirit,

> *"Virginia, write what I am going to reveal to you about my existence before and after speaking the world into existence through my beloved Son. This book will be published and read throughout the entire world for all to know 'I Am' the one and only true God, and no god existed before me or will exist after me.*

> *"No one created me or gave me birth. I always was and always will be. I have the power to speak anything into existence and accomplish whatsoever pleases me. I am always content, happy, and constantly working. I am a God of love, mercy, salvation, and judgment. I create good, and I create evil. I never sleep or get tired. I only rested from all my works after I created the universe and man six thousand years ago."*

"And on the seventh day God finished His work that He had done, and He rested on the seventh day from all His work that He had done" (Genesis 2:2 ESV).

> *"My very first creation was my beloved Son Jesus, whom I created from my inner being with the presence and power of my Holy Spirit, who is always with me. I appointed my son heir to all things, through whom the world was made. (See Hebrews 1:1- 4) I gave commandments to my Son to accomplish my will. He always pleases me and brings me great joy. I delight always in him as he delights always in me. I taught him how to do everything, and we do all things together. I desired to create beings fashioned like my son to be joint-heirs with him in my Kingdom."*

"Now if we are children, then we are heirs-heirs of God and co-heirs with Christ if indeed we share in His sufferings in order that we may also share in His glory" (Romans 8:17 NIV).

"I created all things through my Son according to my divine will. Like the Holy Spirit, he fulfills all my endeavors. In Genesis, I'm speaking to both my Son and the Holy Spirit, saying, 'let us make man in our likeness and image.' I wanted to be one with mankind like I am one with my beloved Son. I created all things through him and for him because I desired a family to love."

"And God said, let us make man in our image, after our likeness: and let them have dominion over the fish of the sea, and over the fowl of the air, and over the cattle, and over all the earth, and over every creeping thing that creepeth upon the earth" (Genesis 1:26 KJV).

"I created laws for mankind to keep and give blessings to those who follow my laws. I place my curse on those who do not obey my commandments. I am a Holy God and cannot sin. When the first-born man Adam was created, and later on his wife, Eve, both were informed to keep my commandments and that disobedience would separate them from me and cause my judgment of death to be upon them. Sin disrupts the good design that I want for mankind's life. I gave free will to all the angels I created and to Adam and Eve and their seed after them. Adam and Eve were both beguiled by Satan, a fallen angel, and chose my judgment of death for them and their seed.

"It is my will that everyone has eternal salvation and not die in their unrepentant sins and have to face eternal damnation in the fires of hell."

"For I have no pleasure in the death of anyone, declares the Lord GOD; so, turn and live" (Ezekiel 18:32 ESV).

"I offered my son's life as atonement for the sins of mankind. He took their punishment by dying on the cross. The only thing one must do is repent of their sins and accept my beloved son, Jesus, as atonement for all their sins."

"For God so loved the world that He gave His one and only Son, that whoever believes in Him shall not perish but have eternal life" (John 3:16 NIV).

"I created everything for my children through my Son, who is in harmony with all my endeavors.

"The Bible gives an account of my creation in Genesis, written by my prophet Moses. Angels were created by my Son and given specific ranks in my heavenly realm. Then, the first man was created, fashioned after my Son, to be joint-heirs with him and live forever in my kingdom." As I breathed life into my beloved Son, He breathed my life force into the first created man, Adam, who was the firstborn of all creation and the beginning of our eternal family."

"For in him (Jesus) all things were created: things in heaven and on earth, visible and invisible, whether thrones or powers or rulers or authorities; all things have been created through Him and for Him" (Colossians 1:16 NIV)

"I gave my Son rulership over those who are saved and judgment on those who are lost. Virginia, you outlined my Ten Commandments in your book, 'Virginia O'Hare

Documents God's Law Vs. Man's Law.' I made that book a best seller and blessed your other books as well. Believers who repent of their sins will live under my son's rulership and go into the 1000-year millennium. After the 1000 years of peace, my Son will turn the kingdom over to me, and I will live forever with those who love me and keep my commandments in their hearts and mind."

"Then the end will come, when He hands over the kingdom to God the Father after He has destroyed all dominion, authority and power" (1 Corinthians 15:24 NIV).

"I always was. I have no beginning and no end. I am the Alpha and the Omega. Before I created the heavens and the earth and the first created beings, Adam and Eve, there existed no one. I am the one and only true and eternal God of the universe. Throughout the centuries, I have chosen certain prophets, as I have chosen you, to give my prophetic word to my people. The Bible records my communion with mankind and my very deep and profound feelings of love and mercy towards all those who turn to me. My wrath is on those who hate me and are in rebellion. I give life, and I take it away according to my will. I give everyone the gift of eternal salvation to those who repent of their sins and accept my son Jesus as their savior.

"The angels were created before I created the first man, Adam. I created myriads of angels and gave each a specific rank. One of the highest-ranking angels created was Lucifer, who was given power, beauty, wisdom, and position above all the other angels in my heavenly realm. He was allowed to hover over my throne and was perfect *in all his ways until pride over his beauty caused iniq-uity to enter him. He wanted to replace me in my King-dom and wanted all the worship angels gave to me. He convinced one-third of all the angels to follow him in his rebellion against me."*

"You were an anointed guardian cherub. I placed you; you were on the holy mountain of God; in the midst of the stones of fire, you walked. You were blameless in your ways from the day you were created, till unrighteousness was found in you. In the abundance of your trade, you were filled with violence in your midst, and you sinned; so I cast you as a profane thing from the mountain of God, and I destroyed you, O guardian cherub, from the midst of the stones of fire" (Ezekiel 28:14-16 ESV).

"Earthly rulers, whether they know it or not, rule in the spirit and under the influence of Satan's wiles. He is the principality behind the powers of this corrupt world sys-tem."

"For we do not wrestle against flesh and blood, but against the rulers, against the authorities, against the cosmic powers over this present darkness, against the spiritual forces of evil in the heavenly places" (Ephesians 6:12 ESV).

CHAPTER ONE

World War III is on the Horizon
Who Will Win?

Earth-shattering events are now occurring globally that are leading mankind to the precipice of disaster. These events are rapidly unfolding with frequency and intensity like never before in world history. God's Final 21 Judgments on humanity will soon explode worldwide.

Before these end-of-the-age prophetic events occur, God is giving humanity a final opportunity to repent of their sins and obey His command to accept His Son, Jesus, as their Lord and Savior. He provides His Son as atonement to everyone for their sins, so they can be washed clean by His atoning blood, shed on the Cross of Calvary. Jesus' death paid the price in full for all of God's judgment on humanity and sin. Upon making a simple confession of faith, one receives eternal salvation in the Kingdom of God, where joy, peace, and happiness await all believers. Those who refuse God's saving grace of salvation will have the fires of hell waiting to embrace them for all eternity. God gives the Good News of eternal life to everyone. Upon taking one's last breath, without accepting God's saving grace of salvation, an eternity of unending and unimaginable pain and suffering in the eternal fires of hell awaits them.

According to God's timetable, the final prophetic events will soon occur and herald in the end of this Satanic age. We are in the countdown to World War III and the beginning of the 7-year tribulation that will end with the Battle of Armageddon. God's final 21 judgments on humanity will be during the 7-year Tribulation and be complete with the commencement of the Battle of Armageddon between God and Satan that will usher in the Second Coming of Jesus Christ and the final elimination of Satan, the Antichrist, the False Prophet, sin, and death. These events are all on the immediate horizon! Very soon, our nation will become involved in an earth-shaking and earth-shattering war that will be fought with major nuclear missiles and cause an indescribable amount of conflagration globally. This war will take the lives of one-third of the world's population.

God destroyed the entire world during Noah's day with the flood. This time, His final judgment on the world will be with fire. Soon, all nations will come against Israel and use their nuclear missiles to try and annihilate the entire Jewish State. This war will cause a third of the world's population to die with countless earthly devastation. To end this war, all warring nations will agree to a seven-year peace treaty, brokered by a very intelligent, charismatic, political leader who will come from a small western European country. The Bible describes this man as having a dark countenance, and Satan himself will empower him. The Bible calls him the Antichrist, a man of lawlessness. He will influence all warring nations to cease battling against Israel and sign a seven-year peace treaty, which he brilliantly composes. **Bible prophecy confirms that the final 7-year tribulation on earth will begin with the signing of this peace treaty.** (See Daniel 9:27)

Halfway through the seven-year peace treaty, the Antichrist will break his agreement with Israel. He will sit in the rebuilt Temple of God to proclaim himself as God and rule all the world's kingdoms with full authority and satanic power. At the end of his three-and-a-half-year reign, he will cause all nations to go to war and again attack Israel. This will cause God to intervene, and the final Battle of Armageddon, between God and Satan, will begin. This is when God will herald in the Second Coming of Jesus Christ, who will be at the helm of this great battle for God and will completely defeat Satan and all the nations that come against Israel. Jesus wins, and Satan loses. Then, while still alive, the Antichrist and the False Prophet will be thrust into the fires of hell forever.

The Bible describes the Antichrist as "the little horn, the beast, the man of lawlessness, and the son of perdition." He will soon come on the political stage as an influential political leader. He will be very charismatic and possess eloquent speech with very persuasive skills. He will implement the globalization of the entire world and do the following:

He will claim to be God and demand worship. "Don't let anyone deceive you in any way, for that day will not come until the rebellion occurs and the man of lawlessness is revealed, the man doomed to destruction. He will oppose and will exalt himself over everything that is called God or is worshiped, so that **he sets himself up in God's temple, proclaiming himself to be God**" (2 Thessalonians 2:3-4 NIV).

He will be Satan incarnate who will blaspheme God. "and he opened his mouth in blasphemies against God, to blaspheme his name and his tabernacle, that is, those who dwell in heaven" (Revelation 13:6 KJV).

He will perform miraculous signs and wonders. "and he doeth great wonders so that he maketh fire come down from heaven on the earth in the sight of men" (Revelation 13:13 KJV).

He will appear to come back to life after a fatal head wound, and the false prophet, a religious leader, heralds in the Antichrist as a savior. "And he exerciseth all the power of the first beast before him, and causeth the earth and them which dwell therein to worship the first beast, whose deadly wound was healed. And he doeth great wonders, so that he maketh fire come down from heaven on the earth in the sight of men, And deceiveth them that dwell on the earth by the means of those miracles which he had the power to do in the sight of the beast; saying to them that dwell on the earth, that they should make an image to the beast, which had the wound by a sword, and did live" (Revelation 13:12-14 KJV).

He will try and duplicate the life of Jesus Christ. Jesus was in His ministry for three and a half years. The Antichrist will be in power for three and a half years. Jesus is the Son of God. The Antichrist is the son of Satan. Jesus Christ died on the cross and was resurrected. The Antichrist will recover from a fatal head wound. After he comes back to life, the false prophet wants an image to be set up of the Antichrist in the rebuilt Temple of God for everyone to honor, just as the Cross honors the resurrected Jesus

The Antichrist will rise to power after an invasion of Israel by the major countries of the world. He will broker a peace treaty with Israel and bordering nations while promising protection for Israel for seven years. The Antichrist will be considered a miracle worker, literally and politically. The world will come to worship him. The signing of this peace treaty will commence at the start of the seven-year tribulation.

After three and a half years of the seven-year peace treaty, the antichrist will break the agreement with Israel. This heralds at the beginning of the last half of the seven-year tribulation, "and there was given unto him a mouth speaking great things and blasphemies; and power was given unto him to continue forty and two months. (Three and a half years) and he opened his mouth in blasphemy against God, to blaspheme His name, His tabernacle, and them that dwell in heaven. And it was given unto him to make war with the saints, and to overcome them: and power was given him over all kindreds, and tongues, and nations. **"for three and a half years he was given authority over every tribe, people, language and nation"** (Revelation 13:5,7 KJV).

He will rule and reign over all the world's nations and make mandatory laws for all to obey. He will be in charge of the world's economy and force his **mark** on everyone's hand or forehead, which is his name or a number, and also force all to worship his image. "forced all people, great and small, rich and poor, free and slave, to receive a mark on their right hands or on their foreheads, so that they could not buy or sell unless they had the mark, which is the name of the beast or the number of its name" (Revelation 13:16-17 KJV).

He will desecrate God's temple in Jerusalem. Jesus warned His disciples, "Therefore when you see the 'abomination of desolation,' spoken of by Daniel the prophet, standing in the holy place" (whoever reads, let him understand), "then let those who are in Judea flee to the mountains. Let him who is on the housetop not go down to take anything out of his house. And let him who is in the field not go back to get his clothes. But woe to those who are pregnant and to those who are nursing babies in those days! And pray that your flight may not be in winter or on the Sabbath. For then there will be great tribulation, such as has not been since the beginning of the world until this time, no, nor ever shall be" (Matthew 24:15-21 NKJV). **At the end of the three and one-half years of the great tribulation will commence the Battle of Armageddon and the Second Coming of Jesus Christ.**

He will seek to annihilate all the Jews at the end of the seven-year tribulation by bringing all nations of the world against Israel. "and I saw the beast, and the kings of the earth, and their armies, gathered together to make war against Him (Jesus) that sat on the horse, and against His army" (Revelation 19:19 KJV).

The Bible describes the traits of the Antichrist as being:

Intelligent	Rev 13:18; Daniel 7:8
Charismatic Speaker	Daniel 7:8; Rev 13:5
Crafty Politician	Daniel 9:27; Rev 17:12, 13, 17
Distinct Physical Appearance	Daniel 7:20
Military Genius	Revelation 4; 17:14; 19:19
Economic Genius	Daniel 11:38
Blasphemer	Revelation 13:6
A Man of Lawlessness	2 Thessalonians 2:8
Selfish, Ambitious, Egotistic	Daniel 11:36, 37; 2 Thess 2:4
Greedy for Possessions	Daniel 11:38
Very Controlling	Daniel 7:25
Self-Exalting Above God	Daniel 11:36; 2 Thess 2:4

While the Antichrist is in power, in the last half of the seven-year tribulation, God will send a delusion to all those who only delight in wickedness and deny God and His son Jesus Christ. They won't recognize the true God from the false god. Instead, they will believe the Antichrist and the false prophet's great signs, including causing fire to come down from heaven to the earth in full view of the people. (See Revelation 13:13) This man of sin will deceive many into worshiping him instead of God. Apostle Paul writes, "The coming of the lawless one will be in accordance with how Satan works. He will use all sorts of displays of power through signs and wonders that serve the lie, and all the ways that wickedness deceives those who are perishing. They perish because they refused to love the truth and so be saved. For this reason, God sends them a powerful delusion so that they will believe the lie and so that all will be condemned who have not believed the truth but have delighted in wickedness" (2 Thessalonians 2:9-12 NIV).

God's wrath will be poured out without measure on all those who take the mark of the beast, the Antichrist. "And the third angel followed them, saying with a loud voice, If any man worships the beast and his image, and receive his mark in his forehead, or in his hand, the same shall drink of the wine of the wrath of God, which is poured out without mixture into the cup of his indignation; and he shall be tormented with fire and brimstone in the presence of the holy angels, and in the presence of the lamb: and the smoke of their torment ascendeth up forever and ever: and they have no rest day nor night, who worship the beast and his image, and whosoever receiveth the mark of his name" (Revelation 14:9-11 KJV).

"Then the beast was captured, and with him the false prophet who worked signs in his presence, by which he deceived those who received the mark of the beast and those who worshiped his image. **These two were cast alive into the lake of fire burning with brimstone**" (Revelation 19:20 KJV).

CHAPTER TWO

God's Final Twenty-One End-of-Days Judgments

The most earth-shattering events of biblical proportions will occur during the seven-year tribulation with God's wrath poured out in His Final Twenty-One End-of-Days Judgments on mankind. World War III is soon to unfold, which will cause one-third of the world's population to be killed.

According to the world population projections, at the end of 2021, the global population was 7,874,965,825. The death toll of one-third of the world's population equates to 2.6 billion people who will lose their lives in the upcoming World War III. God's wrath will be poured out without measure in these last days through His Twenty-One End-of-Days Judgments. They will be divided into three sections, the Seven Seal Judgments, the Seven Trumpet Judgments, and the Seven Bowl Judgments.

World War III will bring our world close to annihilation. From that war will appear a man of dark countenance who will be known worldwide in the political arena as a brilliant international peacemaker who will eventually take over all the world's nations. He will be in charge of a one-world government for the last three and a half years of the seven-year tribulation. This prophecy seems impossible to occur that everyone will be under his rulership. However, he will convince the whole world with his deceptive practices. In Noah's days, he warned the people of the coming worldwide flood that would cover the tallest mountains. No one believed him because up to the day of the flood, it had never rained. So, it will be with this man who the Bible calls the Antichrist. All the leaders of the world will turn their power over to him. Satan will give him his power, authority, and throne.

Satan uses two great earthly kingdoms of the world against Christ and His people. One is political, and the other is religious. Satan uses both to persecute the people of God.

Jesus was a Jew, so the Antichrist, in appearance, could be a Jew. However, the Antichrist rises from the revived Roman Empire, which indicates he could be a gentile and not a Jew. At the beginning of the seven-year tribulation, he comes on the political scene with his peace treaty with Israel and the other warring nations. He will posture himself as the world's political leader in the middle of the seven-year tribulation and take his seat in Israel's rebuilt temple and claim to be God himself. His political career will be for a short-lived seven-year period. For this, the Antichrist will spend an eternity in the lake of fire with the devil and false prophet.

In God's Twenty-One Judgments, all countries who follow the Antichrist to war against Israel will be punished by the wrath of God that will be poured out without measure.

Two thousand years ago, Apostle John recorded the details of the war based on a vision he had from Jesus while He was in prison on the Isle of Patmos, a small Greek island in the Aegean

Sea. At the end of the sixth bowl judgment, God will send His Son, Jesus, to gather all believers who fell asleep (died) in the Lord, then gather those who came through the tribulation. Every believer, dead and alive, will meet Jesus in the air and instantly be given a glorified body at His 2nd Coming. Then, they will return with him to earth to witness His conquest of Satan, the Antichrist, the false prophet, and all the nations with them that came against Israel in the Battle of Armageddon. Jesus will triumph over all of God's enemies using one weapon, the sword that will come out of His mouth. Then all of God's Twenty-One Judgments (the Seven Seal Judgments, the Seven Trumpet Judgments, and the Seven Bowl Judgments) will be fulfilled.

These three series of End-Time Judgments will get more devastating, more violent, and more intense as the End-of-Days grows nearer. All Twenty-One Judgments are connected. The Seven Seal Judgments introduce the Seven Trumpet Judgments. The Seven Trumpet Judgments introduce the Seven Bowl Judgments. Together, God's Twenty-One Judgments will commence with the signing of the seven-year peace treaty, brokered and signed by the Antichrist and all nations that went to war against Israel.

During the Seven Seal Judgments, the following events will occur, the Antichrist comes on the scene, there's warfare, famine, plagues, a devastating earthquake, and many heavenly signs, and the martyrdom of believers in Christ

In the Seven Trumpet Judgments, hail and fire destroy much of the plant life in the entire world, the death of much of the world's sea life, the darkening of the sun and moon, a plague of demonic locusts that will torture the unsaved, and one-third of humanity will be killed.

The Seven Bowl Judgments will cause the following: painful sores that will afflict humanity, the death of every remaining sea creature, rivers turning to blood, the sun's intensifying heat, and great darkness. Then the Antichrist's armies will invade Israel in the Battle of Armageddon.

When Jesus comes back the second time, there will be an earthquake that will be so great, it will destroy up to a quarter of the planet's population—followed by large 100 lb hailstones.

A "Scriptural" Overview of God's Final Twenty-One End-of-Days Judgments During the Seven-Year Tribulation

Seven Seal Judgments

1. The Antichrist comes to conquer
"Now I watched when the Lamb opened one of the seven seals, and I heard one of the four living creatures say with a voice like thunder, 'Come!' And I looked, and behold, a white horse! And its rider had a bow, and a crown was given to him, and he came out conquering, and to conquer" (Revelation 6:1-2 ESV).

2. Open warfare breaks out
"When he opened the second seal, I heard the second living creature say, 'Come!' And out came another horse, bright red. Its rider was permitted to take peace from the earth so that people should slay one another, and he was given a great sword" (Revelation 6:3-4 ESV).

3. World famine
"When he opened the third seal, I heard the third living creature say, 'Come!' And I looked, and behold, a black horse! And its

rider had a pair of scales in his hand. And I heard what seemed to be a voice in the midst of the four living creatures, saying, 'A quart of wheat for a denarius, and three quarts of barley for a denarius, and do not harm the oil and wine!'" (Revelation 6:5-6 ESV)

4. One-fourth of the earth's population dies

"When he opened the fourth seal, I heard the voice of the fourth living creature say, 'Come!' And I looked, and behold, a pale horse! And its rider's name was Death, and Hades followed him. And they were given authority over a fourth of the earth, to kill with sword and with famine and with pestilence and by wild beasts of the earth" (Revelation 6:7-8 ESV).

5. Believers call for vengeance

"When he opened the fifth seal, I saw under the altar the souls of those who had been slain for the word of God and for the witness they had borne. They cried out with a loud voice, 'O Sovereign Lord, holy and true, how long before you will judge and avenge our blood on those who dwell on the earth?' Then they were each given a white robe and told to rest a little longer until the number of their fellow servants and their brothers should be complete, who were to be killed as they had been" (Revelation 6:9-11 ESV)..

6. Planetary and celestial disturbances

"When he opened the sixth seal, I looked, and behold, there was a great earthquake, and the sun became black as sackcloth, the full moon became like blood, and the stars of the sky fell to the earth as the fig tree sheds its winter fruit when shaken by a gale. The sky vanished like a scroll that is being rolled up, and every mountain and island was removed from its place. Then the kings of the earth and the great ones and the generals and the rich and the powerful, and everyone, slave and free, hid themselves in the caves and among the rocks of the mountains, calling to the mountains and rocks, 'Fall on us and hide us from the face of him who is seated on the throne, and from the wrath of the Lamb, for the great day of their wrath has come, and who can stand?'" (Revelation 6:12-17 ESV)

7. Initiation of the Seven Trumpets

"When the Lamb opened the seventh seal, there was silence in heaven for about half an hour. Then I saw the seven angels who stand before God, and seven trumpets were given to them. And another angel came and stood at the altar with a golden censer, and he was given much incense to offer with the prayers of all the saints on the golden altar before the throne, and the smoke of the incense, with the prayers of the saints, rose before God from the hand of the angel. Then the angel took the censer and filled it with fire from the altar and threw it on the earth, and there were peals of thunder, rumblings, flashes of lightning, and an earthquake" (Revelation 8:1-5 ESV).

Seven Trumpet Judgments

1. One-third of the earth's remaining vegetation is destroyed

"Now the seven angels who had the seven trumpets prepared to blow them. The first angel blew his trumpet, and there followed hail and fire, mixed with blood, and these were thrown upon the earth. And a third of the earth was burned up, and a third of the trees were burned up, and all green grass was burned up" (Revelation 8:6-7 ESV).

2. One-third of the earth's remaining sea life is destroyed

"The second angel blew his trumpet, and something like a great mountain, burning with fire, was thrown into the sea, and a third of the sea became blood. A third of the living creatures in the sea died, and a third of the ships were destroyed" (Revelation 8:8-9 ESV).

3. One-third of the earth's fresh water supply is contaminated
"The third angel blew his trumpet, and a great star fell from heaven, blazing like a torch, and it fell on a third of the rivers and on the springs of water. The name of the star is Wormwood. A third of the waters became wormwood, and many people died from the water because it had been made bitter" (Revelation 8:10-11 ESV).

4. One-third of the heavens goes dark
"The fourth angel blew his trumpet, and a third of the sun was struck, and a third of the moon, and a third of the stars, so that a third of their light might be darkened, and a third of the day might be kept from shining, and likewise a third of the night" (Revelation 8:12 ESV).

5. Swarms of satanic locusts are released from the pits of hell
"And the fifth angel blew his trumpet, and I saw a star fallen from heaven to earth, and he was given the key to the shaft of the bottomless pit. He opened the shaft of the bottomless pit, and from the shaft rose smoke like the smoke of a great furnace, and the sun and the air were darkened with the smoke from the shaft. Then from the smoke came locusts on the earth, and they were given power like the power of scorpions of the earth. They were told not to harm the grass of the earth or any green plant or any tree, but only those people who do not have the seal of God on their foreheads. They were allowed to torment them for five months, but not to kill them, and their torment was like the torment of a scorpion when it stings someone. And in those days people will seek death and will not find it. They will long to die,

but death will flee from them. In appearance the locusts were like horses prepared for battle: on their heads were what looked like crowns of gold; their faces were like human faces, their hair like women's hair, and their teeth like lions' teeth; they had breastplates like breastplates of iron, and the noise of their wings was like the noise of many chariots with horses rushing into battle. They have tails and stings like scorpions, and their power to hurt people for five months is in their tails" (Revelation 9:1-12 ESV).

6. One-third of the earth's remaining population is killed

"Then the sixth angel blew his trumpet, and I heard a voice from the four horns of the golden altar before God, saying to the sixth angel who had the trumpet, 'Release the four angels who are bound at the great river Euphrates.' So the four angels, who had been prepared for the hour, the day, the month, and the year, were released to kill a third of mankind. The number of mounted troops was twice ten thousand times ten thousand; I heard their number. And this is how I saw the horses in my vision and those who rode them: they wore breastplates the color of fire and of sapphire and of sulfur, and the heads of the horses were like lions' heads, and fire and smoke and sulfur came out of their mouths" (Revelation 9:13-17 ESV).

7. Introduction of the Seven Bowls

"Then the seventh angel blew his trumpet, and there were loud voices in heaven, saying, 'The kingdom of the world has become the kingdom of our Lord and of His Christ, and He shall reign forever and ever.' And the twenty-four elders who sit on their thrones before God fell on their faces and worshiped God, saying, 'We give thanks to you, Lord God Almighty, who is and who was, for you have taken your great power and begun to reign. The nations raged, but your wrath came, and the time for the dead to be judged, and for rewarding your servants, the prophets and saints, and those who fear your name, both small and great, and for destroying the destroyers of the earth.' Then God's temple in heaven was opened, and the ark of His covenant was seen within His temple. There were flashes of lightning, rumblings, peals of thunder, an earthquake, and heavy hail" (Revelation 11:15-19 ESV).

Seven Bowl Judgments

1. Painful sores on those who follow the Antichrist
"Then I heard a loud voice from the temple telling the seven angels, 'Go and pour out on the earth the seven bowls of the wrath of God.' So the first angel went and poured out his bowl on the earth, and harmful and painful sores came upon the people who bore the mark of the beast and worshiped its image" (Revelation 16:1-2 ESV).

2. The earth's remaining sea life is destroyed
"The second angel poured out his bowl into the sea, and it became like the blood of a corpse, and every living thing died that was in the sea" (Revelation 16:3 ESV).

3. The earth's remaining freshwater is destroyed
"The third angel poured out his bowl into the rivers and the springs of water, and they became blood. And I heard the angel in charge of the waters say, 'Just are you, O Holy One, who is and who was, for you brought these judgments. For they have shed the blood of saints and prophets, and you have given them blood to drink. It is what they deserve!' And I heard the altar saying, 'Yes, Lord God the Almighty, true and just are your judgments!'" (Revelation 16:4-7 ESV)

4. The earth's remaining population is scorched with fire

"The fourth angel poured out his bowl on the sun, and it was allowed to scorch people with fire. They were scorched by the fierce heat, and they cursed the name of God who had power over these plagues. They did not repent and give Him glory" (Revelation 16:8-9 ESV).

5. Darkness falls over all of the earth

"The fifth angel poured out his bowl on the throne of the beast, and its kingdom was plunged into darkness. People gnawed their tongues in anguish and cursed the God of heaven for their pain and sores. They did not repent of their deeds" (Revelation 16:10-11 ESV).

6. The Battle of Armageddon commences

"The sixth angel poured out his bowl on the great river Euphrates, and its water was dried up, to prepare the way for the kings from the east. And I saw, coming out of the mouth of the dragon and out of the mouth of the beast and out of the mouth of the false prophet, three unclean spirits like frogs. For they are demonic spirits, performing signs, who go abroad to the kings of the whole world, to assemble them for battle on the great day of God the Almighty. ('Behold, I am coming like a thief! Blessed is the one who stays awake, keeping his garments on, that he may not go about naked and be seen exposed!') And they assembled them at the place that in Hebrew is called Armageddon" (Revelation 16:12-16 ESV).

7. A great earthquake destroys all that remains

"The seventh angel poured out his bowl into the air, and a loud voice came out of the temple, from the throne, saying, 'It is done!' And there were flashes of lightning, rumblings, peals of thunder, and a great earthquake such as there had never been since man was on the earth, so great was that earthquake. The great city was split into three parts, and the cities of the nations fell, and God remembered Babylon the great, to make her drain the cup of the wine of the fury of his wrath. And every island fled away, and no mountains were to be found. And great hailstones, about one hundred pounds each, fell from heaven on people; and they cursed God for the plague of the hail because the plague was so severe" (Revelation 16:17-21 ESV).

God's Twenty-One End-of-Days Judgments fall on all the wicked nations of the world. After Jesus's victory in the Battle of Armageddon, He scatters the bodies of the wicked across the earth. Then God sends the birds to eat the flesh of all the bodies. "Then I saw an angel standing in the sun, and with a loud voice he called to all the birds that fly directly overhead, 'Come, gather for the great supper of God, to eat the flesh of kings, the flesh of captains, the flesh of mighty men, the flesh of horses and their riders, and the flesh of all men, both free and slave, both small and great" (Revelation 19:17-18 ESV).

Each of these Twenty-One Judgments creates multiple implications in their fulfillment. The Seals, Trumpets, and Bowl Judgments are God's wrath on sin, Satan, and the Antichrist's kingdom of wickedness.

No one knows the day or the hour when Christ returns, but every believer will know the season. We are the generation who will witness these major world events that will lead the entire world into the seven years of tribulation and the end of our world that is now under Satan's rulership.

Confirmation of these end-time events was also given to Prophet Daniel in a visitation from Archangel Gabriel, who explained to Daniel what would befall his people at the end-of-days. The Book of Daniel begins in 604 B.C. and ends two years after the seventy years of exile in 532 B.C. The first six chapters detail historical records; the last six chapters detail Daniel's visions.

Daniel's prophetic message and interpretation from Arch Angel Gabriel:

"At that time shall arise, Michael, the great prince who has charge of your people. And there shall be a time of trouble, such as never has been since there was a nation till that time. But at that time your people shall be delivered, everyone whose name shall be found written in the book. And many of those who sleep in the dust of the earth shall awake, some to everlasting life, and some to shame and everlasting contempt. And those who are wise shall shine like the brightness of the sky above; and those who turn many to righteousness, like the stars forever and ever. But you, Daniel, shut up the words and seal the book, until the time of the end. Many shall run to and fro, and knowledge shall increase. Then I, Daniel, looked, and behold, two others stood, one on this bank of the stream and one on that bank of the stream. And someone said to the man clothed in linen, who was above the waters of the stream, 'How long shall it be till the end of these wonders?' And I heard the man clothed in linen, who was above the waters of the stream; he raised his right hand and his left hand toward heaven and swore by him who lives forever that it would be for a time, times, and half a time, and that when the shattering of the power of the holy people comes to an end all these things would be finished. I heard, but I did not understand. Then I said, 'O my lord, what shall be the outcome of these things?' He said, 'Go your way, Daniel, for the words are shut up and sealed until the time of the end. Many shall purify themselves and make themselves white and be refined, but the wicked shall act wickedly. And none of the wicked shall understand, but those who are wise shall understand. And from the time that the regular burnt offering is taken away and the abomination that makes desolate is set up, there shall be 1,290 days. Blessed is he who waits and arrives at the 1,335 days. But go your way till the end. And you shall rest and shall stand in your allotted place at the end of the days" (Daniel 12:1-13 ESV).

Chapter Summary
We are now waiting for God's sixth trumpet judgment, the start of World War III, which will take the lives of one-third of the world's population and cause worldwide devastation. World War III will end with the Antichrist emerging and brokering a seven-year peace treaty with Israel, that will commence the seven-year tribulation. He will come into the political arena, which will commence the beginning of the seven-year tribulation. In the last three and a half years of the seven-year tribulation, he will be in full control of a One-World Global Government. After which, he will lead all the countries into the Battle of Armageddon. He will have satanic powers to dictate laws that will take away the constitutional rights of the people. He will cause all to agree to his legislation, and no one will be able to buy or sell unless they take his mark, which the bible calls the mark of the beast. "And he causeth all, both small and great, rich and poor, free and bond, to receive a mark in their right hand, or in their foreheads: And that no man might buy or sell, save he that had the mark, or the name of the beast, or the number of his name." (Revelation 13:16-17 KJV).

The Antichrist will be at the helm of governments all over the world with the full power and throne of Satan. He will make laws that cause all to take his mark on their hand or forehead to worship him. This man, like Satan, will crave worship and power. He will be obsessed with self-adulation. At the end of his three-and-a-half-year reign, he will start the most unholy war of all time by bringing all the world's armies against Israel. This is the last act of a desperate Satanic force, which will herald in the Second Coming of Jesus, who will defeat Satan, the Antichrist, and all the nations that come against God and Israel.

Warning to All: If anyone takes the mark of the beast, they will spend an eternity in the lake of fire with the Antichrist and the false prophet! I caution everyone, don't take the mark of the beast!!! The antichrist will enforce this mark and not allow anyone without his mark to buy or sell anything, including necessities, homes, food, clothing, or any form of possession. There will be serious consequences for those who refuse to take his mark on their hand or forehead. He will make it mandatory for all to get his mark. However, if anyone takes his mark, they will be showing signs of worshipping the Antichrist over God. The Bible says God's wrath will be on all those who worship the Beast and take his mark. "A third angel followed them and said in a loud voice: 'If anyone worships the beast and its image and receives its mark on their forehead or on their hand, they, too, will drink the wine of God's fury, which has been poured full strength into the cup of his wrath. They will be tormented with burning sulfur in the presence of the holy angels and of the Lamb. And the smoke of their torment will rise forever and ever. There will be no rest day or night for those who worship the beast and its image, or for anyone who receives the mark of its name" (Revelation 14:9-11 NIV).

The Antichrist will deceive the world by performing miracles like making fire come down from heaven to convince people to worship him and that he is the world's savior. Only Jesus, the Son of God, is our Savior and not some beast that gets his power from God's adversary, Satan, the Devil. All true Christians, saved by the Blood of Jesus, will not be deceived. The Holy Spirit will bring into every believer the Truth of God and Jesus Christ to refuse the mark of the beast. Those beguiled by this Antichrist, like Adam and Eve were in the Garden of Eden by Satan, will face eternal torment in the fires of hell and be tormented day and night forever if they take the mark of the Antichrist. We must trust in God and His son Jesus Christ and seek first the kingdom of God. That is where we all need to spend our eternity, not in the eternal fires of hell.

CHAPTER THREE

End of Days Events
Are Now Converging

Today, tensions are mounting astronomically around the world, with fears rising over the dangerous and countless calamities that are exploding around the globe. Many countries now possess dangerous chemical and biological warfare and nuclear bombs that can annihilate our entire planet. Recently, powerful missiles were used to attack Israel. This country rightfully retaliated and defended its country and the lives of its citizens by using their powerful state-of-the-art missiles. Natural disasters are now covering the globe costing billions of dollars to repair the infrastructure, including communication networks, sewage, water, electric systems, and transportation systems vital to a country's economic development systems.

With each country trying to increase the destructive power of their nuclear missiles, there is no question that the human race could come close to extinction. Our entire civilization is now in jeopardy as world leaders continue to accumulate more powerful nuclear missiles in their arsenal. This is especially dangerous when there is so much dissension and disagreement among world leaders.

One very powerful nuclear bomb created by the United States, called "Castle Yankee," tested to be more than thirteen megatons. This one bomb alone expels a radiation mushroom cloud with a height of more than 40 km and a diameter of more than 16 km. It emits a radiation cloud that can reach the capital of Mexico within four days. Such mushroom-shaped clouds were described in the Book of Revelation by Apostle John as an end-time sign that would occur in the sky before the Second Coming.

The Day of the Lord

"Blow the trumpet in Zion, and sound an alarm in my holy mountain! Let all the inhabitants of the land tremble; For the day of the Lord is coming, For it is at hand: A day of darkness and gloominess, A day of clouds and thick darkness, Like the morning clouds spread over the mountains. A people come, great and strong, The like of whom has never been; Nor will there ever be any such after them, Even for many successive generations. A fire devours before them, And behind them a flame burns" (Joel 2:1-3 NKJV).

Fire, smoke, and thick gloomy darkness are a description fitting for a nuclear explosion. A nuclear missile exchange between two major countries like Russia and America could cause an earthquake and a mushroom cloud of debris and ash to rise. "I watched as he opened the sixth seal. There was a great earthquake. The sun turned black like sackcloth made of goat hair, the whole moon turned blood red, and the stars in the sky fell to earth, as figs drop from a fig tree when shaken by a strong wind. The heavens receded like a scroll being rolled up, and every mountain and island was removed from its place" (Revelation 6:12-14 NIV). Being a first-century Christian, Apostle John was writing down what he saw and what knowledge he possessed two thousand years ago.

However, greater than man's nuclear weapons is God's supernatural power. He can make anything happen, including stars falling from the sky and moving mountains and islands out of their places. It is estimated that there are one hundred billion stars in our milky way, and God has a name for each star. "He decides how many stars there should be. He gives each one of them a name" (Psalm 147:4 NIRV).

Jesus warned His apostles of these prophetic signs and wonders that would occur before His Second Coming, which includes the near extinction of all humanity. Regardless of how serious these natural end-of-days disasters become, they will not occur until the Gospel is preached throughout the entire inhabited world and everyone has been given the Gospel message. Then, and only then, will God send His Son to gather all His "elect," and bring them home to God's Kingdom.

Who are the "elect?" They're everyone, dead or alive, who repented of their sins and made Jesus Christ their Lord and Savior. Those who refuse to accept this offer of salvation through Jesus will have to pay the penalty for their own sins and spend an eternity in the fires of hell. No one needs to go to hell for their sins. Just know that Jesus paid for every sin ever committed on the Cross of Calvary. All one has to do is repent and accept God's gift of salvation through His Son, Jesus Christ. It's that simple. No amount of good works, or good deeds, or any religious organization, will get you into heaven outside of our Savior, Jesus Chris, who confirms: "I am the way, the truth, and the life. No one comes to the Father except through me" (John 14:6 NIV) Jesus Christ died for our sins so we wouldn't have to pay the penalty of eternal damnation in the fires of hell. Instead, God offers His son as an atonement for all of mankind's sins. Why? Because He loves every one of us that much. "For God so loved the world that He gave His one and only Son, that whoever believes in him shall not perish but have eternal life" (John 3:16 NIV).

Time is running out! The signs are all here and are global. They include plagues, pandemics, and pestilences that cause fatal diseases like the Bubonic Plague, Ebola, and Coronavirus and its variants. As of October 2021, more than 4.8 million people have died from the Coronavirus, and there have been more than 236 million cases in 220 countries and territories. There are new and more deadly plagues surfacing in diverse places in our world. The World Health Organization (WHO) has added another Covid strain to its list of coronavirus variants: the Covid-19 lambda variant, which has spread to more than two dozen countries. On November 24, 2021, a new variant of SARS-CoV-2, B.1.1.529, (Omicron,) was reported to the World Health Organization (WHO); Omicron positives are doubling nearly every two days. This new variant was first detected in specimens collected on November 11, 2021 in Botswana and on November 14, 2021 in South Africa.

God mentions a plague He will put on people who wage war on Jerusalem, and describes the symptoms of the plague in this scripture: "And this shall be the plague with which the Lord will strike all the peoples that wage war against Jerusalem: their flesh will rot while they are still standing on their feet, their eyes will rot in their sockets, and their tongues will rot in their mouths" (Zechariah 14:12 ESV).

Who are the people that will wage war against Jerusalem? The Lord said a ten-nation coalition would assemble in the last days. One is the country of Rosh which is north of Israel. In the Bible, geographical directions are given in conjunction with the State of Israel. Therefore, when Ezekiel and Daniel both describe one of Israel's end-time aggressors as the "King of the North," that country, north of Israel, can only be modern-day Russia. (see Daniel 11:5-35)

Russia has the largest landmass in the world of 11.0%, almost twice the size of Canada, which has 6.1%. Israel, in comparison, has a total land area of 8,367 sq. miles. The size of Israel is comparable to New Jersey. Israel has had more controversy over its land and people than any country in the world. Ezekiel's prophecy lends support to Daniel's prophecy of invading armies against Israel in the last days. *"You will come from your place out of the uttermost parts of the north, you and many peoples with you, all of them riding on horses, a great host, a mighty army. You will come up against my people Israel, like a cloud covering the land. In the latter days I will bring you against my land, that the nations may know me, when through you, O Gog, I vindicate my holiness before their eyes"* (Ezekiel 38:15-16 ESV). Modern-day Russia matches the description of being north of Israel.

Ezekiel 38:1-39 details the final battle, in the last days, between God and Satan. The following scripture mentions the countries that will attack Israel in the final war at the end of the seven-year tribulation. The Bible calls this the Battle of Armageddon. (see Chapter Six of this book) *"The word of the Lord came to me: 'Son of man, set your face toward Gog, of the land of Magog, the chief prince of Meshech and Tubal, and prophesy against him and say, Thus says the Lord God: Behold, I am against you, O Gog, chief prince of Meshech and Tubal. And I will turn you about and put hooks into your jaws, and I will bring you out, and all your army, horses and horsemen, all of them clothed in full armor, a great host, all of them with buckler and shield, wielding swords. Persia, Cush, and Put are with them, all of them with shield and helmet; Gomer and all his hordes; Beth-Togarmah from the uttermost parts of the north with all his hordes—many peoples are with you"* (Ezekiel 38:1-6 ESV).

Two thousand five hundred years ago, God foretold Ezekiel that in the latter days, Israel would be restored, which it was on May 14, 1948, and that the country of Gog, chief prince of Meshech and Tubal, would lead the invasion against Israel. He said this would occur at the end of the seven-year tribulation. Gog (Russia) will be allied with several Islamic nations, Persia (Iran), Cush, and Put, who hate Israel and want to wipe the country out of existence. Other countries mentioned in Ezekiel 38 that will join Russia and attack Israel are Ethiopia, Sudan, Gomer, Togarmah (Turkey), and Libya. God said He would gather all the nations of the world to the Battle of Armageddon. *"In those days and at that time, when I restore the fortunes of Judah and Jerusalem, I will gather all nations and bring them down to the Valley of Jehoshaphat. There I will put them on trial for what they did to my inheritance, my people Israel, because they scattered my people among the nations and divided up my land"* (Joel 3:1-2 NIV).

Even though Iran, Sudan, and Libya will join Russia and Turkey, other Arab states and countries could also be involved. Satan will assemble, through the Antichrist, the kings of the whole world to battle against God in the Battle of Armageddon. "For they are demonic spirits, performing signs, who go abroad to the kings of the whole world, to assemble them for battle on the great day of God the Almighty" (Revelation 16:14 ESV). When all the nations of the world come against Israel, it is on that day that God will send His son to go out and fight against those nations.

Chapter Summary

Living in this world today is one big battle after another. In each believer's life, our battles are fought and won by our Lord and Savior, Jesus Christ! One major battle our country is facing is poverty. Statistics show the number of people living below the poverty line in the United States in 2019 is about 34 million. In 2020 it was estimated that about 2% of the world's population were homeless. Terrorists are another battle our country is facing. Terrorists around the world are causing the destruction and deaths of innocent men, women, and children. They ruthlessly murder a countless number of innocent people with their evil attacks. Immorality is another major battle peaking like the days of Sodom and Gomorrah and the days of Noah. Jesus compared the days of Noah before the flood, when He spoke to His apostles, in His "Olivet 'Discourse" of end-time signs before His Second Coming. "As it was in the days of Noah, so it will be at the coming of the Son of Man" (Matthew 24:37 NIV). He warned of earthquakes, hurricanes, and natural disasters that would increase with frequency and intensity before His 2nd coming and said things would be so wicked that like in Noah's days' men's thoughts in their hearts were only evil continually. *The Lord saw how great the wickedness of the human race had become on the earth, and that every inclination of the thoughts of the human heart was only evil all the time. The Lord regretted that He had made human beings on the earth, and His heart was deeply troubled. So the Lord said, 'I will wipe from the face of the earth the human race I have created—and with them the animals, the birds and the creatures that move along the ground—for I regret that I have made them"* (Genesis 6:5-7 NIV).

God caused a flood to destroy every human being except for eight people, Noah, a righteous God-fearing preacher, and his entire family. God instructed Noah to build an ark for him and his family and all the animals he wanted in the ark.

Today, our world is filled with the same wickedness. What will God do to our generation for man's wickedness? If He destroyed the earth with a flood that covered the tallest mountain in Noah's day, what would God do today to our sinned-filled world?

Today, God is giving us a spiritual ark, His Son Jesus Christ, to be protected from His wrath and judgment. To get into this spiritual ark, all one has to do is repent of all their sins and accept Jesus as your Savior.

We know what happened to the non-believers in God during Noah's flood. This is what Apostle Peter says will happen to those in the end-of-days. "But the day of the Lord will come like a thief. The heavens will disappear with a roar; the elements will be destroyed by fire, and the earth and everything done in it will be laid bare. Since everything will be destroyed in this way, what kind of people ought you to be? You ought to live holy and godly lives as you look forward to the day of God and speed its coming. That day will bring about the destruction of the heavens by fire, and the elements will melt in the heat. But in keeping with His promise we are looking forward to a new heaven and a new earth, where righteousness dwells" (2 Peter 3:10-13 NIV).

CHAPTER FOUR

Current Prophetic Signs of Upheavals in the U.S. and Globally

Due to all the upheavals facing the world today, there doesn't appear to be any respite from major calamities. Instead, they are increasing with frequency and intensity. There's global unrest as countries try to deal with insurmountable problems such as:

A decline of natural resources, water being at the top of the list

Population growth beyond earth's carrying capacity

Global warming

Chemical pollution that's affecting our atmosphere

Oceans rising

The unchecked proliferation of nuclear weapons of mass destruction

Biological weapons, which include natural toxins and pathogens, like coronavirus, anthrax bacterium, and delta variant

These prophetic signs of the last days are causing fear, unrest, confusion, and taking their toll on humanity and the economy around the world.

Prophetic events in 2020 of the ten biggest natural disasters in our world:

The Australian bushfires

Devastating floods in Indonesia

Volcano eruption in the Philippines

Multiple hurricanes in the United States

Earthquakes in Turkey, the Caribbean, China, Iran, Russia, the Philippines, and India

Locust swarms in East Africa, parts of India, and Asia

A cyclone in India and Bangladesh

A windstorm in Europe

Major floods in India, Japan, and China

The snow turning green in Antarctica

As governments face these endless challenges worldwide, calamities continue to increase with record-breaking intensity. Human existence is in a crisis mode dealing with:

Natural disasters damaging our infrastructures

Illegal immigration, which is up 71%.

A lack of affordable health care with our federal budget deficit.

Increased violent crime with unchecked lawlessness.

International terrorism.

The unemployment rate in the U.S. is now 4.8% (*September 2021*).

Climate change is affecting the country's economic and financial stability.

COVID-19

Global plagues, pandemics, and pestilence are prophetic signs of the end-of-days. On November 17, 2019, the first detectable case of the deadly and very contagious coronavirus surfaced in Wuhan, China. This virus rapidly spread across the globe and became a worldwide pandemic that affected a large portion of the world's population. As of October 2021, there have been over 4,900,000 Coronavirus deaths. Millions more worldwide have been exposed. Our government calls for mandatory restrictions. Travel is one of them. A new variant of the Coronavirus, the Delta Variant, is now present in all fifty states and accounts for 52% of new infections in the United States.

The death toll from Coronavirus and its variants is rising, causing an unbelievable lifestyle change for the world. Currently, government restrictions include a six-foot social distancing, wearing gloves, face masks, being quarantined for an unspecified period, and staying away from crowds. The government is encouraging everyone to take the vaccines to cope with this pandemic with no guarantees, only medical assumptions to encourage all to be vaccinated. Social distancing is required during church services, schools, universities, restaurants, sporting events, theaters, weddings, and hospitals, which only allow one person to visit for births, emergency surgeries, and chronic illnesses. These restrictions are mostly without exceptions. This pandemic has affected countless business owners across our country in having to downsize the number of customers they can service due to complying with the six-foot social distancing and other required restrictions.

Large corporations are also affected by these mandatory restrictions and find it very challenging. Some are complying to safeguard the health and well-being of their employees and customers, while others, not opposing the vaccine but challenge the mandatory mandates, as affecting their constitutional rights through the Courts. Everyone's normal routine has been dramatically disrupted or altered. Most everyone has developed alternative ways to cope with taking these essential health measures.

In addition to dealing with natural disasters and the Coronavirus and its variants, major Executive Orders are being made by the new administration. On January 20, 2021, President Joe Biden signed an executive order halting the southern border wall construction and promised amnesty for millions of immigrants to come into the United States. This order has opened the door to illegal immigration, which has created countless major humanitarian crises. One is a lack of resources to accommodate the number of immigrants. The burst of population growth from the influx of this immigration requires humane care of their needs, which is not being done. Their need for housing, food, health care, and medical needs are just a few of the social and humanitarian problems our government is now facing. The spread of the Coronavirus and other variants of the disease is a major health crisis surfacing throughout these immigrants' crowded encampment. One example is, 354 people in one pod that should only accommodate 33. This Executive Order has also opened the door to the escalation of criminal activity such as drug cartels, human and child trafficking, which is abhorrent.

Another Executive Order signed by President Biden was to shut down the Keystone XL Pipeline. This has caused gas shortages and increased gas prices. American's are now facing inflation with rising prices on almost all goods. For decades, inflation has averaged under 2% for the typical American. Suddenly, inflation is rising much faster. The latest government data in March 2022 showed prices rose 8.3%, the highest in more than three decades, as measured by the Consumer Price Index (CPI). Other inflation metrics also have shown significant increases in recent months, though not to the same extent as the CPI. Every citizen's worse fears are materializing while facing one calamity after another. Stress is paramount, while stability is crumbling. Living with all these problems with no solutions in sight is challenging for the American people. For any nation to survive, God is, and always has been the number one answer. What we all should do is pray to God, as He is the only hope for our lives, families, and country.

> Dear God,
>
> We pray for our nation. Strengthen and defend us in all our daily battles. Help us fight for our country by being good citizens and being part of the solutions. Keep safe our families and the Godly values we hold dear. We pray for our people that we may grow united in love and appreciation for who we are in you and your Son, Jesus Christ, our Lord, and Savior.
>
> Amen

The American People are Protesting for their Constitutional Rights:

On Wednesday, January 6, 2021, the United States Capitol in Washington, D.C., was stormed during a riot with a violent attack against the U.S. Congress. These were supporters of President Donald Trump, who attempted to overturn his defeat in the 2020 Presidential Election by disrupting the joint session of Congress, who were assembled to count the electoral votes to formalize President-Elect Joe Biden's victory. Cries of voter fraud permeated all over the news media.

Looting and rioting in our streets over police brutality is another real and major problem facing our country today. Heightened with crowds screaming, "Discrimination, Racism, and Black Lives Matter!" Our citizen's rights are being challenged. Many feel that some of our civil and constitutional rights are being diminished as well as our God-given rights as American citizens. Fighting for our civil liberties has been escalated into high gear since the murder of George Floyd by police officers. His death only heightened awareness of how long police officers have violated their oath of office to protect American citizens' civil and constitutional rights. Too often, our judicial system gives officers qualified immunity for their criminal behavior.

One death caused by any police officer against an American citizen, unjustly, is one death too many!!! Every guilty officer should be held accountable. Our judicial system too often overlooks an officer's criminal behavior and ignores their victims' legal, civil, and constitutional rights. Families have to carry to their grave the injustice caused to their loved ones who were unjustly accused while being victims of police brutality.

Upon every police officer's employment, they take their oath of office: "I do solemnly swear (or affirm), that I will support the Constitution of the United States, and the Constitution and laws of the state of _______, that I will bear true faith and allegiance to the same, and defend them against enemies, foreign and domestic, and that I will faithfully and impartially discharge the duties of a peace officer, to the best of my ability, so help me God."

Every officer who violates this oath of office should be brought to justice without qualified immunity.

Christ said increased lawlessness was one of the final prophetic signs of the last days. "And because lawlessness will be increased, the love of many will grow cold. But the one who endures to the end will be saved" (Matthew 24:12-13 ESV).

Jesus also warned His apostles that in addition to lawlessness proliferating before His Second Coming, there would be natural earthly upheavals that would increase worldwide. Today, unlike ever before in world history, everyone is witnessing all the signs and conditions merging, exactly like the Bible predicted would occur just before the Second Coming of Jesus.

For Sale and Help Wanted signs are on almost every commercial street corner in America. Many owners are closing their doors due to operating at a loss since the Coronavirus restrictions were enacted. With the stimulus package, the government pays workers more to stay home than their earnings from working. This is hurting businesses who want to hire them. As this world continues to go into a tailspin, there doesn't seem to be any recovery in sight. Every day there seem to be more and more upheavals surfacing throughout the world. Two thousand years ago, prophets predicted these events would occur just before the Second Coming of Jesus.

The soon coming of Jesus is good news for those who repented of their sins and accepted Him as their Lord and Savior. In the meantime, our hope and faith in God will see every one of us through these turbulent last-days birth pains. It is essential for everyone to keep their faith strong in God and not in this world. Those days will be shortened for the elect's sake when they are raptured out of this God-forsaken world by Jesus. Until then, even though turbulent times will increase with frequency and intensity, our faith in God will see us through every adversity with triumphs.

We must keep our minds focused on God's promise that He will never leave or forsake us. "Keep your life free from love of money, and be content with what you have, for He promises, 'I will never leave you nor forsake you'" (Hebrews 13:5 ESV). So, no matter what we are going through, we have the greatest power in the universe who resides in every one of us, and that is our Heavenly Father! Jesus told His apostles, "Do you not know that you are God's temple and that God's Spirit dwells in you? If anyone destroys God's temple, God will destroy him. For God's temple is holy, and you are that temple" (1 Corinthians 3:16-17 ESV). The truth of this blessed assurance will see us through the most trying times we are all living through.

Everyone must know we all possess our unalienable rights given to each one of us by God. Since 1787, congress has ratified twenty-seven amendments to our Constitution. They protect our freedom of speech, freedom of the press, freedom of assembly, freedom of petition, and freedom to worship God. Congress cannot create a national religion. So, as of today, we still have freedom of religion. God's Commandment is to love Him and each other. He created us as His eternal family. In His Ten Commandments, His first commandment is to love Him. We must remember that no matter what we or this world goes through, we must keep God in first place in our hearts and minds and always love him. God gives each of us the blessed assurance that we have an inheritance waiting for us in heaven. This life will soon end but God, who loves us unconditionally, has rewards waiting for us through His Son, Jesus Christ. All we need to do is believe, have faith, and repent of our sins then God will give each of us a life that the eye has not seen nor ear has heard nor has it entered into the heart of man what God has in store for those who love him. "But as it is written, Eye hath not seen, nor ear heard, neither have entered into the heart of man, the things which God hath prepared for them that love him" (1 Corinthians 2:9 KJV).

No matter what is ahead for this world, God has us safe and secure in the spiritual ark of His Son, Jesus Christ, our Lord, and Savior. He will never leave or forsake us. For those who have not as yet accepted Jesus as their Lord and Savior and have not repented of their sins, all they have is today and now. When they die, eternal damnation awaits them in the fires of hell. To encourage people to believe in God's Gospel of Salvation through Him, Jesus spoke about hell during His three and a half years of ministry. In the New Testament, there are 162 references to hell. Over 70 of those references were spoken of by Jesus Christ. Going to hell is something everyone should avoid. Jesus promises every believer heaven on earth and warns, "I have said these things to you, that in me you may have peace. In the world you will have tribulation. But take heart; I have overcome the world" (John 16:33 ESV).

Jesus accomplished salvation for you and me when He died on the Cross of Calvary for the sins of the whole world. No one should give up this awesome inheritance in heaven in exchange for an eternity in the fires of hell!

CHAPTER FIVE

Only God Knows the Day and Hour of Jesus' Second Coming!

Jesus's disciples asked Him, "Tell us, when will these things be, and what will be the sign of your coming and the end of the age?" "He said, "But of that day and hour knoweth no man, no, not the angels of heaven, but my Father only" (Matthew 24:36 KJV). He told His disciples what the final sign would be, "And this gospel of the kingdom shall be preached in all the world for a witness unto all nations; and then shall the end come" (Matthew 24:14 KJV). What is the Gospel? In Christianity, the Gospel is the Good News of salvation for all of mankind, upon the imminent coming of the Kingdom of God through the atonement of Jesus Christ on the cross, His resurrection from the dead brings reconciliation between God and everyone who repents of their sins and accepts Jesus as their Lord and Savior.

These scriptures are etched in the Word of God for everyone to know He gives His offer of eternal salvation to everyone through His Son, Jesus Christ:

John 3:16 KJV
"For God so loved the world, that He gave His only begotten Son, that whosoever believeth in him should not perish, but have ever-lasting life."

John 3:36 KJV

"He that believeth on the Son hath everlasting life: and he that believeth not the Son shall not see life, but the wrath of God abideth on him."

Romans 10:9 KJV

"That if thou shalt confess with thy mouth the Lord Jesus, and shalt believe in thine heart that God hath raised him from the dead, thou shalt be saved."

1 John 5:12 KJV

"He that hath the Son hath life, and he that hath not the Son of God hath not life."

We are witnessing the Gospel being preached throughout the entire inhabited world today through every available media source, including the internet, radio, tv, news magazines, and this book's publication. Today, we are witnessing all the end-of-days prophetic signs converging together at once. Jesus said these signs would occur just before His Second Coming. These signs are now rapidly materializing in front of our very eyes as we watch the twenty-four-hour breaking news stories from around the world. It's exciting and thrilling to be a believer knowing we will soon enter the Kingdom of God as believers who kept their faith in Jesus. We have the Blessed Assurance we have the only way to heaven, through our Lord and Savior, Jesus Christ. "Jesus saith unto him, I am the way, the truth, and the life: no man cometh unto the Father, but by me" (John 14:6 KJV).

All one needs to do is repent of their sins and accept God's gift of salvation through His Son, Jesus Christ. It's that simple. No amount of good works, or good deeds, or any religious organization, will get anyone into heaven outside of Jesus. Apostle John confirms this, "For God so loved the world, that He gave

His only Son, that whoever believes in him should not perish but have eternal life. For God did not send His Son into the world to condemn the world, but so that the world might be saved through him. Whoever believes in him is not condemned, but whoever does not believe is condemned already, because he has not believed in the name of the only Son of God. And this is the judgment: the light has come into the world, and people loved the darkness rather than the light because their works were evil. For everyone who does wicked things hates the light and does not come to the light, lest his works should be exposed. But whoever does what is true comes to the light, so that it may be clearly seen that his works have been carried out in God" (John 3:16-21 ESV).

Jesus Christ died for our sins on the Cross of Calvary, so we wouldn't have to pay the penalty for our own sins in the eternal fires of hell that were prepared by God for the fallen angels. Because God loves us, He gave His own Son as atonement for mankind's sins.

Additional signs of Jesus's Second Coming are earthquakes and other natural disasters that will increase with frequency and intensity before His Coming to earth to rapture His elect. Since 1950, the number of earthquakes per decade has doubled every ten years. In recent studies, the number of other natural and geo-physical disasters like volcanoes, dry rock-falls, landslides, and avalanches has also increased. The average number and cost to infrastructure are in the billions of dollars and are on the rise.

Not since the days of Noah has the world been so badly battered as it is in our generation. Jesus said to His disciples, "All these are but the beginning of the birth pains" Matthew 24:8 ESV). A woman in labor has birth pains that increase with frequency and intensity until the baby is born. Jesus compares His Second Coming to a woman in labor. Believers are going through the tribulations Jesus said we would have to endure until He comes. "These things I have spoken unto you, that in me ye might have peace. In the world ye shall have tribulation: but be of good cheer; I have overcome the world" (John 16:33 KJV). The end-of-days signs are increasing with such rapid succession. Soon, God will send His Son through the clouds to rapture all believers, both dead and alive.

In the United States alone, we have outbreaks of rioting in our streets, protesting against injustice and violations of our civil and constitutional rights. Police brutality and racial discrimination are at the core of these uprisings. This has opened Pandora's Box to terrorists and looters and has cost multi-billions of dollars in damages, affecting companies, businesses, property, and infrastructures. Our government faces very serious issues, with a lack of bipartisan support and cooperation between our elected officials seeking solutions to these major problems. Lawlessness is escalating in our country as well as around the globe. The United States-Mexico border has seen migrant crossings increase by 71%, bringing into our country increased crime, corruption, and disease.

Discord is high among leaders of foreign countries who possess powerful nuclear bombs. This presents a real threat to life on our planet. There's also the real threat of a cyber attack on the United States power grid, which we are unprepared to handle. This would affect all sectors of the US economy that make up the nation's infrastructure and rely on electricity. This would do serious harm to our nation as a whole. These are real looming threats to survival facing our country today, with the reality of

World War III that could break out at any time. Bible prophecy confirms there will be an army of 200,000,000 forces marching against Israel. Never before in recorded history has our world been prepared for war with such a militia as we have today.

God has richly blessed the United States of America because our Founding Fathers created our country's Constitution on the belief of one God, the Bible, and the Ten Commandments. On July 30, 1956, "In God, We Trust" became the nation's motto. The United States of America dominates economic and military power throughout the world. As God gave the nation of Israel power over their enemies, God has given the United States of America power over her enemies. Our 45th president, Donald J. Trump, honored God, the Bible, and Israel during his administration. He recognized Jerusalem as the Capital of Israel and moved our embassy to Jerusalem. This was a milestone leap for our country politically to recognize Jerusalem as the Capital of Israel. This move pleased God, who promised: "I will bless those who bless you, and whoever curses you I will curse, and all peoples on earth will be blessed through you" (Genesis 12:3 NIV).

Jesus personally gave His divine words to His apostles for every one of us to read concerning the events that would occur just before He comes. Everyone needs to read the entire chapter of Matthew 24 to realize our days here on earth are truly numbered:

Matthew 24:1-51 (NIV)
"Jesus left the temple and was walking away when His disciples came up to him to call His attention to its buildings. 'Do you see all these things?' He asked. 'Truly I tell you, not one stone here will be left on another; everyone will be thrown down.'

As Jesus was sitting on the Mount of Olives, the disciples came to him privately. 'Tell us,' they said, 'when will this happen, and what will be the sign of your coming and the end of the age?'

Jesus answered: 'Watch out that no one deceives you. For many will come in my name, claiming, 'I am the Messiah,' and will deceive many. You will hear of wars and rumors of wars but see to it that you are not alarmed. Such things must happen, but the end is still to come. Nation will rise against nation, and kingdom against kingdom. There will be famines and earthquakes in various places. All these are the beginning of birth pains.

'Then you will be handed over to be persecuted and put to death, and you will be hated by all nations because of me. At that time many will turn away from the faith and will betray and hate each other, and many false prophets will appear and deceive many people. Because of the increase of wickedness, the love of most will grow cold, but the one who stands firm to the end will be saved. And this gospel of the kingdom will be preached in the whole world as a testimony to all nations, and then the end will come.

'So when you see standing in the holy place 'the abomination that causes desolation,' spoken of through the prophet Daniel—let the reader understand—then let those who are in Judea flee to the mountains. Let no one on the housetop go down to take anything out of the house. Let no one in the field go back to get their cloak. How dreadful it will be in those days for pregnant women and nursing mothers! Pray that your flight will not take place in winter or on the Sabbath. For then there will be great distress, unequaled from the beginning of the world until now—and never to be equaled again.

'If those days had not been cut short, no one would survive, but for the sake of the elect, those days will be shortened. At that time if anyone says to you, 'Look, here is the Messiah!' or, 'There he is!' do not believe it. For false messiahs and false prophets will appear and perform great signs and wonders to deceive, if possible, even the elect. See, I have told you ahead of time.

'So if anyone tells you, 'There he is, out in the wilderness,' do not go out; or, 'Here he is, in the inner rooms,' do not believe it. For as lightning that comes from the east is visible even in the west, so will be the coming of the Son of Man. Wherever there is a carcass, there the vultures will gather.

'Immediately after the distress of those days 'the sun will be darkened, and the moon will not give its light; the stars will fall from the sky, and the heavenly bodies will be shaken.'

'Then will appear the sign of the Son of Man in heaven. And then all the peoples of the earth will mourn when they see the Son of Man coming on the clouds of heaven, with power and great glory. And He will send His angels with a loud trumpet call, and they will gather his elect from the four winds, from one end of the heavens to the other.

'Now learn this lesson from the fig tree: As soon as its twigs get tender and its leaves come out, you know that summer is near. Even so, when you see all these things, you know that it is near, right at the door. Truly I tell you, this generation will certainly not pass away until all these things have happened. Heaven and earth will pass away, but my words will never pass away.

'But about that day or hour no one knows, not even the angels in heaven, nor the Son, but only the Father. As it was in the days of Noah, so it will be at the coming of the Son of Man. For in the days before the flood, people were eating and drinking, marrying and giving in marriage, up to the day Noah entered the ark; and they knew nothing about what would happen until the flood came and took them all away. That is how it will be at the coming of the Son of Man. Two men will be in the field; one will be taken and the other left. Two women will be grinding with a hand mill; one will be taken and the other left.

'Therefore keep watch, because you do not know on what day your Lord will come. But understand this: If the owner of the house had known at what time of night the thief was coming, he would have kept watch and would not have let his house be broken into. So you also must be ready, because the Son of Man will come at an hour when you do not expect him.

'Who then is the faithful and wise servant, whom the master has put in charge of the servants in his household to give them their food at the proper time? It will be good for that servant whose master finds him doing so when he returns. Truly I tell you, he will put him in charge of all his possessions. But suppose that servant is wicked and says to himself, 'My master is staying away a long time,' and he then begins to beat his fellow servants and to eat and drink with drunkards. The master of that servant will come on a day when he does not expect him and at an hour he is not aware of. He will cut him to pieces and assign him a place with the hypocrites, where there will be weeping and gnashing of teeth.'"

Jesus is warning every one of us to be ready for His Second Coming because we don't know the day or the hour of His return. We should live each day like it could be our last because we do not know when we will take our last breath here and our next breath in front of Jesus to be judged as either a believer or a non-believer.

CHAPTER SIX

The Battle of Armageddon

Our world is now experiencing the final birth pains of the end-of-days and the end of Satan's rulership of planet earth. This will occur when he is defeated by Jesus in the Battle of Armageddon. That is when God will send His angel down from heaven to grab hold of Satan, chain him, and throw him into the bottomless pit and lock him in for 1000 years.

"Then I saw an angel coming down from heaven. He had in his hand a key to the hole without a bottom. He also had a strong chain. He took hold of the dragon, that old snake, who is the Devil, or Satan, and chained him for 1,000 years. The angel threw the devil into the hole without a bottom. He shut it and locked him in it. He could not fool the nations anymore until the 1,000 years were completed" (Revelation 20:1-3 NLV).

Until then, Satan seeks to utterly destroy the entire human race. He hates humanity because God created us in His likeness and image. He will cause havoc, chaos, and mayhem in every-ones' life, up to and including his final battle with God in the Battle of Armageddon. Satan will use his power and try everything he can to avoid his inevitable end. The Bible says he will form an unholy alliance with two men, one called the Antichrist, and a pseudo-religious leader called the false prophet. He mimics God's Holy Trinity with these two men as his unholy trinity. He empowers them with his demonic plan to try and destroy God and the entire human race. We can see these catastrophes happening now worldwide. Jesus confirmed Satan's plan and said, "And unless the Lord had shortened those days, no flesh would be saved; but for the elect's sake, whom He chose, He shortened the days" (Mark 13:20 NKJV).

Before God created Adam and Eve, Satan wanted everything God possessed, including His power, majesty, and worship from all His angels. His obsession now in these final days is to deceive the nations and fulfill his diabolical plan to cause death and earthly destruction globally to the entire human race. To accomplish this, Satan will give his power, authority, and throne over to the Antichrist. He uses the false prophet to deceive the nations and proclaim to the world that the Antichrist, who recovers from a fatal head wound during the seven-year tribulation, is a diety. The false prophet will have an image erected of the Antichrist to be worshipped in God's Holy Temple in Jerusalem. The Bible calls this act the Abomination of Desolation. "And forces shall be mustered by him, and they shall defile the sanctuary fortress; then they shall take away the daily sacrifices, and place there the abomination of desolation" (Daniel 11:31 NKJV).

The Antichrist will convince political leaders worldwide to use their powerful nuclear weaponry to annihilate Israel. Satan knows God's chosen people reside there, and this is where God will set up his earthly throne during the 1000-year millennium.

Through his unholy trinity with the Antichrist and the False Prophet, Satan will soon cause World War III to occur by turning all the nations of the world against Israel. This devastating, all-out war will cause one-third of the world's population to be killed. After that, Satan will empower the Antichrist to broker and design a masterfully written seven-year peace treaty with Israel and the nations that warred against Israel. This treaty will be brilliantly composed to please all the world leaders, who will herald the Antichrist as a brilliant politician. All these world leaders will so admire him as the peacemaker and savior of humanity that they will turn their power of leadership over to him. This peace treaty fulfills Daniel's seventieth week prophesy, "And he shall confirm the covenant [peace treaty] with many for one week [7 years]: and in the midst of the week [3 1/2 years], he shall cause the sacrifice and the oblation to cease, And for the overspreading of abominations he shall make it desolate, even until the consummation, and that determined shall be poured upon the desolate" (Daniel 9:27 KJV).

After the signing of the peace treaty, there will be world peace for the first 3 1/2 years of the 7-year tribulation. At the beginning of the last 3 1/2 years of the 7-year tribulation, the Antichrist will break the peace treaty with Israel, which he brilliantly brokered among the nations. Then, he alone will be in full control of all world affairs while being led by Satan himself.

He will relish this powerful role and want everyone to worship him. In Jesus's Revelation to John, He refers to the Antichrist as "the Beast from the abyss" (See John 11:7) and "The Beast from the sea." (See John 13:1). In 2 Thessalonians 2:1-12, he is called the "man of sin" and "son of perdition." The Antichrist will come to power during a time of general apostasy and deceive people with signs and wonders. He will sit in the Temple of God and even claim to be God. The last three and a half years of the Antichrist's reign will be so horrific for the world it's called the "Great

Tribulation. He will exercise satanic powers over the entire world. He will be assassinated with a deadly head wound, then miraculously come back to life. This is when the false prophet heralds him as God incarnate and wants everyone to worship him. To further deceive the people, he will have the false prophet cause fire to come down from heaven as a means to further deceive people into worshiping him. "He performs great signs so that he even makes fire come down from heaven on the earth in the sight of men" (Revelation 13:13 NKJV).

During the middle of the seven-year tribulation, the Antichrist dies from a fatal head wound and miraculously comes back to life. He mimics Christ dying on the Cross of Calvary and being divinely resurrected by His Father. After that, one of the Antichrist's first actions is to break his peace treaty with Israel. Then he desecrates the newly rebuilt Holy Temple by setting himself up as God. The false prophet will force everyone to worship the Antichrist, and no one will be allowed to buy or sell unless they take his mark on their hand or forehead. "It also forced all people, great and small, rich and poor, free and slave, to receive a mark on their right hands or on their foreheads" (Revelation 13:16 NIV).

The Antichrist will issue a decree to kill the entire Jewish population. Only one-third of the Jews will make it safely out of Jerusalem and flee into the desert. Then, this Satanic-inspired Antichrist will kill three of the ten kings in power. The remaining seven kings will turn their power over to him. The Antichrist will rule the world for the last three and a half years of the seven-year tribulation. This is the same amount of time Jesus spent in His earthly ministry. The Antichrist's reign during the last three and a half years of the tribulation is called the "Great Tribulation."

This is because there will be such great distress, unequaled from the beginning of the world until then, and never to be equaled again.

The Antichrist plans to destroy the Jews by bringing his armies unexpectedly down on Jerusalem. This will once again put Jerusalem under gentile control. This is when the Jewish people will earnestly repent of their sins and pray for their messiah, Jesus Christ, to return to save them.

Jesus answers their prayers and returns to earth to defeat the armies of the Antichrist, fighting them without human assistance. He will only use the words of His mouth to defeat them all easily! The Antichrist and his armies will be slain by Jesus, the true savior of mankind. The good news is that Satan will be defeated by Jesus.

What will we be doing, after coming back to earth with Jesus as resurrected Saints, while He fights in the Battle of Armageddon? First, we will be riding white horses and be dressed in fine linen, clean and white. "The armies of heaven were following him, riding on white horses and dressed in fine linen, white and clean" (Revelation 19:14 NIV).

Our garments are white and clean because we will only be witnesses to this great battle, not physically fighting in it. It's only Jesus whose garments will be stained with blood, and His only weapon will be a double-edged sword coming out of His mouth. "In His right hand He held seven stars, and coming out of His mouth was a sharp, double-edged sword. His face was like the sun shining in all its brilliance" (Revelation 1:16 NIV). We will also witness Satan being chained by an angel who will throw him into the bottomless pit for 1000 years.

Armageddon is in the plain of Megiddo in the fertile Jezreel Valley and is considered the jewel in the crown of Biblical archaeology. It's the most important land route in the ancient near east and the site for international trade for thousands of years. Epic battles were fought there during the Biblical period, including the Canaanites, Egyptians, Israelites, Assyrians, Persians, and the Englishmen in the modern era. Megiddo is the only site in Israel mentioned by every great power in the ancient near east. For thousands of years, this location has been renowned for battles between good and evil.

The full Biblical picture of the glorious return of our Lord and Savior, Jesus Christ, returning and triumphantly defeating the three unholy members of the satanic trinity, the Dragon (Satan), the Beast (the Antichrist), and the False Prophet (pseudo-religion) is revealed in Revelation 19.

"I saw heaven standing open and there before me was a white horse, whose rider is called Faithful and True. With justice, He ((Jesus) judges and wages war. His eyes are like blazing fire, and on His head are many crowns. He has a name written on him that no one knows but He himself. He is dressed in a robe dipped in blood, and His name is the Word of God. The armies of heaven were following him, riding on white horses and dressed in fine linen, white and clean. Coming out of His mouth is a sharp sword with which to strike down the nations. 'He will rule them with an iron scepter.' He treads the winepress of the fury of the wrath of God Almighty. On His robe and on His thigh He has this name written: KING OF KINGS AND LORD OF LORDS. And I saw an angel standing in the sun, who cried in a loud voice to all the birds flying in midair, 'Come, gather together for the great supper of God, so that you may eat the flesh of kings, generals, and the mighty, of horses and their riders, and the flesh of all people, free and slave, great and small.' Then I saw the beast and the kings of the earth and their armies gathered together to wage war against the rider on the horse and His army. But the beast was captured and with it the False Prophet who had performed the signs on its behalf. With these signs, he had deluded those who had received the mark of the beast and worshiped its image. The two of them were thrown alive into the fiery lake of burning sulfur. The rest were killed with the sword coming out of the mouth of the rider on the horse, and all the birds gorged themselves on their flesh" (Revelation 19:11-21 NIV).

Immediately after Satan's defeat, and the destruction of the Antichrist and all his forces, Jesus will go and stand on the Mount of Olives in a symbolic victory ascent. There will be many supernatural cataclysmic events that will come upon the whole earth. The greatest earthquake of all time will occur. Jerusalem will be split into three areas, and the Mount of Olives will be split into two parts, which will create a valley. There will be hailstorms, and the sun and moon will not give their light. These worldwide catastrophes occur at the end of the last seven-year Tribulation and the Battle of Armageddon. They accompany Jesus' Victory and His global judgment. (See Zechariah 14:3-5; Joel 3:14-16; Matthew 24:29; Revelation 16:17-21).

This will be the end of all evil on the face of this earth and in the entire universe. Life in God's Kingdom will be a place all believers can and will live eternally in peace, harmony, and love. No longer will we have to deal with the evil perpetrated by Satan, his demons, and his followers. There will be no more poverty, stress, anxiety, sickness, frailties, crime, corruption, hunger, thirst, hospitals, poverty, minorities, or racial discrimination. Death and tears will be swallowed up forever!

"He will swallow up death forever, And the Lord God will wipe away tears from all faces; The rebuke of His people He will take away from all the earth; For the Lord has spoken" (Isaiah 25:8 NKJV).

CHAPTER SEVEN

What Happens to Believers at Jesus' Second Coming?

At Jesus' Second Coming, He will first be at the helm of this great war between God and Satan, which will occur at the end of the seven-year tribulation. Jesus will appear in the sky with all His angels and have them gather together all those who accepted him before taking their last breath. Then, every believer alive, who lived through the tribulation and refused to take the mark of the beast, will be caught up together in the sky to meet Jesus and those who were resurrected from their sleep. Everyone, in the twinkling of an eye, will be instantly changed from their corruptible body to a new incorruptible and glorified body. Their new body will be imperishable, sin-free, with the same attributes of Jesus's glorified body.

There will be an enormous amount of joy and gladness while rejoicing with families and loved ones during this long-awaited reunion. Everyone will recognize each other, even with their new bodies. None of those believers raptured was appointed to God's wrath. His wrath is only on those who refused to accept Him and His Son, Jesus, as their Lord and Savior. The unsaved will have a great deal of fear, knowing their eternal judgment will be in the fires of hell, and will instinctively know it's too late to repent of their sins and accept God's Son as atonement for their sins. They will want the mountains to literally fall on them to hide from the wrath of God. "And said to the mountains and rocks, Fall on us, and hide us from the face of Him that sitteth on the throne, and from the wrath of the Lamb" (Revelation 6:16 KJV).

God's wrath will be against all the nations that come against Israel and His chosen people. God is offering His grace to the world, so we don't have to ever experience His wrath for our sins. Those who reject His grace as atonement for their sins through His Son, Jesus, will experience His wrath and judgment in the eternal fires of hell. Satan and his demons are moving across the globe more noticeably today than ever before in world history. They will continue to corrupt our entire world. Satan and his demons use their evil diabolical powers to destroy God's laws and His offer of salvation to the entire human race. The Bible explains this is because we are in the final countdown to the end of Satan's rulership of planet earth. He knows he has a short time left before he's chained and thrown into the bottomless pit for a thousand years. He wants to take all of humanity to follow him into his bottomless abode for a thousand years.

At the end of the thousand-year millennium, all non-believers will face God's Judgment Seat at the Great White Throne Judgment. They will have to answer for their own sins and take their just punishment in the eternal lake of fire. After taking their last breath, it will be too late to accept Jesus as their atonement for their sins.

"Then I saw a great white throne and him who was seated on it. From His presence, earth and sky fled away, and no place was found for them. And I saw the dead, great and small, standing before the throne, and books were opened. Then another book was opened, which is the book of life. And the dead were judged by what was written in the books, according to what they had done. And the sea gave up the dead who were in it, Death and Hades gave up the dead who were in them, and they were judged, each one of them, according to what they had done. Then Death and Hades were thrown into the lake of fire. This is the second death, the lake of fire. And if anyone's name was not found written in the book of life, he was thrown into the lake of fire" (Revelation 20:11-20 ESV).

Satan has no power in hell. He is not the "ruler" in hell but a captive, just as are all those who didn't accept God's free gift of eternal salvation by repenting of their sins and believing in the finished work of Jesus Christ on the cross.

While Satan will be chained in the bottomless pit for a thousand years, every believer will be Raptured into God's Kingdom and safely reside there, and be gloriously happy for a thousand years, free from all of Satan's evil and demonic wiles.

CHAPTER EIGHT

What Happens After The Battle of Armageddon?

After the Battle of Armageddon, the most important occurrence for every believer in Jesus Christ is eternal salvation. Everyone will reside joyfully and eternally in God's Kingdom here on earth for one thousand years. There will be joy and happiness that's unimaginable among those saved as they reunite with their saved loved ones and family. After that, God will create a new heaven and a new earth, and the former things will pass away. There will be a great celebration of the unbelievable beauty God created for those who love him. Everyone will marvel at their new glorified bodies without all the pain and infirmities one experiences in this earthly body. These new and glorified bodies feel so free and un-encumbered. It will be thrilling to be in a body that feels so wonderful. Our life will be indescribably beautiful in God's Kingdom. There are no words that can describe what our life will be like in heaven. It's unspeakable, but this author, with the prompting of the Holy Spirit, will give an accurate account, so everyone will know what God meant when He said, "Eye has not seen, nor ear heard, Nor have entered into the heart of man The things which God has prepared for those who love Him" (1 Corinthians 2:9 NKJV).

Everyone will be free from all the evil poured upon their lives and planet earth by the evil one, Satan. Sin and death will be swallowed up forever. Believers will be reunited with all their saved loved ones. They will be thrilled to be in their glorified bodies, free from pain, anguish, sin, and death. God will wipe away everyone's tears. Each believer will have a glorified body like Jesus that is not restricted to time or space. Amazing things will happen after we are raptured and changed into our heavenly bodies, which will be in the twinkling of an eye. We will have the most delicious food, pastries, wine, cheese, meat, and every good thing. We will inhabit our own homes, mortgage-free. We will never have to pay any bills. There will be no hospitals or nursing homes. No one will age!!!

Now the non-believers and Satan, the devil, will not be so fortunate. Read their fate in Revelation 20.

"And I saw an angel coming down out of heaven, having the key to the Abyss and holding in his hand a great chain. He seized the dragon, that ancient serpent, who is the devil, or Satan, and bound him for a thousand years. He threw him into the Abyss and locked and sealed it over him, to keep him from deceiving the nations anymore until the thousand years were ended. After that, he must be set free for a short time.

I saw thrones on which were seated those who had been given authority to judge. And I saw the souls of those who had been beheaded because of their testimony about Jesus and because of the word of God. They had not worshiped the beast or its image and had not received its mark on their foreheads or their hands. They came to life and reigned with Christ for a thousand years. (The rest of the dead did not come to life until the thousand years were ended.) This is the first resurrection. Blessed and holy are those who share in the first resurrection. The second death has no power over them, but they will be priests of God and Christ and will reign with him for a thousand years.

The Judgment of Satan

When the thousand years are over, Satan will be released from his prison and will go out to deceive the nations in the four corners of the earth—Gog and Magog—and to gather them for battle. In number, they are like the sand on the seashore. They marched across the breadth of the earth and surrounded the camp of God's people, the city He loves. But fire came down from heaven and devoured them. And the devil, who deceived them, was thrown into the lake of burning sulfur, where the beast and the false prophet had been thrown after their defeat in the Battle of Armageddon. They will be tormented day and night forever and ever.

The Judgment of the Dead

Then I saw a great white throne and Him who was seated on it. The earth and the heavens fled from His presence, and there was no place for them. And I saw the dead, great and small, standing before the throne, and books were opened. Another book was opened, which is the book of life. The dead were judged according to what they had done as recorded in the books. The sea gave up the dead that were in it, and death and Hades gave up the dead that were in them, and each person was judged according to what they had done. Then death and Hades were thrown into the lake of fire. The lake of fire is the second death. Anyone whose name was not found written in the book of life was thrown into the lake of fire" (Revelation 20:1-15 NIV).

CHAPTER NINE

Jesus Christ Judges Both Believers And Non-Believers

Jesus Christ is coming very soon as our Savior and our Judge. God is leaving Judgments-of-Mankind to His Son. There will be two judgments, one for believers in Christ and one for non-believers. Believers will face Christ's judgment for their crowns and rewards for their good deeds. They will have to give an account of themselves to God, but this does not affect their salvation. They will not be judged for their sins because Jesus paid the penalty for their sins on the Cross of Calvary. Therefore, no believer will be condemned for any of their sins. There is no condemnation for believers, only rewards for good works. "Therefore, there is now no condemnation for those who are in Christ Jesus" (Romans 8:1 NIV).

There are five heavenly "Crowns" believers can receive. They are the Imperishable Crown, the Crown of Rejoicing, the Crown of Glory, the Crown of Righteousness, and the Crown of Life. God offers humanity the awesome gift of His unconditional love, and an incredible life with Him in a world He created for all those who love Him. "But as it is written, Eye hath not seen, nor ear heard, neither have entered into the heart of man, the things which God hath prepared for them that love him" (1 Corinthians 2:9 KJV).

God is offering all believers the following Crowns as rewards for their good deeds done here on earth:

The Imperishable Crown

This Crown is given to believers who faithfully run the race, crucify every selfish desire in the flesh, and point men to Jesus. God calls some people to do things that will require sacrifice in the way they will live and conduct their lives. Some people may be called to be a missionary in a far-off country. They will be working for almost nothing on earthly terms. They will have to sacrifice the money, possessions, and lifestyle they could have had if they stayed home in their own country. The Bible says, "And everyone who competes for the prize is temperate in all things. Now they do it to obtain a perishable crown, but we for an imperishable crown" (1 Corinthians 9:25 NKJV).

This verse implies that these people will receive this crown for the sacrifices they were willing to make to complete the call and mission He had called them to do. Run whatever race God has set out for you and be the best you can be for God. Be willing to make whatever sacrifices that may need to be made to complete the mission that God has set out for you.

The Crown of Rejoicing

This Crown is given to those who faithfully witness God's saving grace and lead souls to Jesus. This Crown has also been named the soul winner's crown. It indicates that God will reward those who have witnessed to others and lead people to Christ. Telling others about the grace of God, telling others about Jesus, is the greatest thing that you can do for someone while here on this earth. When you help lead someone to the Lord, you have just been used as a vessel of God. It says in the bible, "For what is our hope, or joy, or crown of rejoicing? Is it not even you in the presence of our Lord Jesus Christ at His coming?" (1 Thessalonians 2:19 NKJV)

God will judge you by your willingness and desire to be used by Him to witness to others, not necessarily on how many get saved. We are to plant the seed and water it, but only God will make it grow. "I planted the seed, Apollos watered it, but God has been making it grow. So neither the one who plants nor the one who waters is anything, but only God, who makes things grow. The one who plants and the one who waters have one purpose, and they will each be rewarded according to their own labor" (1 Corinthians 3:6-8 NIV). God will fit opportunities for you in your life to witness and work for Him if you allow Him to. Some could be your unsaved friends, family members, or co-workers.

The Crown of Glory
This is the pastor's Crown and will be given to the ministers who faithfully feed the flock of God. This includes preachers, teachers, Sunday school teachers, missionaries, and all those who teach the Word of God in their respective ministries. This Crown signifies the importance of bringing others up into the ways of God. God wants those who are saved to grow and learn as much as they can about Him, His Son, and His Holy Spirit. To do that, He uses mature believers who are willing to teach others.

The Bible says, "To the elders among you, I appeal as a fellow elder and a witness of Christ's sufferings who also will share in the glory to be revealed: Be shepherds of God's flock that is under your care, watching over them—not because you must, but because you are willing, as God wants you to be; not pursuing dishonest gain, but eager to serve; not lording it over those entrusted to you, but being examples to the flock. And when the Chief Shepherd (Jesus) appears, you will receive the crown of glory that will never fade away" (1 Peter 5:1-4 NIV).

The Crown of Righteousness
This Crown is given to those who anxiously await and look forward to the day when He will return for His saints. If you are a believer, you have been made righteous before God the Father as a result of Jesus dying on the cross for all of our sins. This means that the righteousness of Jesus has now been imputed to you. It also refers to us living a good and righteous life for God the Father with what time we have left down here. It says in the Bible, "Now there is in store for me the crown of righteousness, which the Lord, the righteous Judge, will award to me on that day—and not only to me but also to all who have longed for his appearing" (2 Timothy 4:8 NIV).

There are Christians who are righteous before God the Father as a result of being saved by the blood of Jesus Christ, but they are not living righteous lives in their actions, words, and behaviors. Some people may be saved in God's eyes but continue to do evil works that the unsaved would do. We all have our flaws, weaknesses, and certain temptations with which we may struggle. It is not perfection but rather direction that God is looking for. God wants each one of us to choose to do the right thing when faced with certain choices. Living a righteous life for God will be rewarding as you are given this Crown by God Himself once you enter heaven.

The Crown of Life
Jesus says that He will give this Crown to those who undergo severe hardship, testing, tribulation, and/or physical death on His

behalf. To be willing to die for your faith in God will be considered the ultimate sacrifice. It is the greatest act of courage and love that you can show God. Christians who have been martyred for their faith throughout history will not only be given this Crown of Life but other rewards once they enter into Heaven. The Bible says, "Blessed is the one who perseveres under trial because, having stood the test, that person will receive the crown of life that the Lord has promised to those who love Him" (James 1:12 NIV).

God blesses those who persevere through trials in this life which builds patience, character, courage, and faith in the one who overcame the world. We must count it all joy when we are in tribulation because we have the blessed assurance that Christ will overcome our battles with His victory. "Blessed is the man who remains steadfast under trial, for when he has stood the test he will receive the crown of life, which God has promised to those who love Him" (James 1:12 ESV).

2 Corinthians 5:10 ESV
"For we must all appear before the judgment seat of Christ, so that each one may receive what is due for what he has done in the body, whether good or evil."

Romans 8:1 ESV
"There is therefore now no condemnation for those who are in Christ Jesus."

2 Timothy 4:8 NIV
"Now there is in store for me the crown of righteousness, which the Lord, the righteous Judge, will award to me on that day—and not only to me but also to all who have longed for His appearing."

1 Peter 5:4 NIV

"And when the Chief Shepherd appears, you will receive the crown of glory that will never fade away."

Revelation 2:10 NIV

"Do not be afraid of what you are about to suffer. I tell you, the devil will put some of you in prison to test you, and you will suffer persecution for ten days. Be faithful, even to the point of death, and I will give you life as your victor's crown."

Matthew 16:27 KJV

"For the Son of man shall come in the glory of His Father with His angels, and then He shall reward every man according to his works."

Non-believers will face a much different judgment from the White Throne Judgment Seat of God. They will be awakened to meet God face to face to answer for their sins. They will only receive condemnation as a penalty for their sins, with no rewards or crowns for their good deeds because they rejected God's Son as their Savior. They will be judged for every single sin they ever committed. And then be cast into the lake of fire. "And I saw a great white throne, and Him that sat on it, from whose face the earth and the heaven fled away; and there was found no place for them. And I saw the dead, small and great, stand before God; and the books were opened: and another book was opened, which is the book of life: and the dead were judged out of those things which were written in the books, according to their works. And the sea gave up the dead which were in it, and death and hell delivered up the dead which were in them: and they were judged every man according to their works. And death and hell were cast into the lake of fire. This is the second death. And whosoever was not found written in the book of life was cast into the lake of fire" (Revelation 20:11-15 KJV).

According to the Bible, the only way to avoid the Great White Throne Judgment is to accept Jesus Christ as your personal Savior. Whether one believes or not, no one escapes death and judgment! The Bible is abundantly clear on God's Judgment of Mankind for either life or death. Everyone should choose life, repent of their sins, and accept the gift of salvation God offers to all of us through His Son Jesus. All of mankind should do this before taking their last breath. After that, it will be too late.

If one accepts Jesus before death, they will know for sure they will spend eternity in heaven on earth. Saying this simple prayer with your heart will guarantee you will go to heaven when you die.

Lord Jesus,

I repent of all my sins and accept you as my Lord and Savior

Amen.

After repenting of your sins and saying this prayer, you made the necessary confession and acceptance of Jesus Christ as an atonement for your sins. You just secured your salvation and will go to heaven. This is a promise from God Almighty, who can not lie. He tells us to repent and live, "For I take no pleasure in the death of anyone, declares the Sovereign Lord. Repent and live!" (Ezekiel 18:32 NIV)

It's appointed once for everyone to die, and then there's judgment. No one takes anything from this world when they die except their sins if they are a non-believer or their works as believers. God gave mankind free will to decide as to where one will spend eternity. God does not send anyone to hell. Man, alone, chooses his destiny as to where he will spend eternity with his free will.

It's only by repenting of ones' sins and accepting God's amazing grace of salvation through His Son, Jesus Christ, can one be saved. God's gift of salvation can not be purchased or earned. This amazing grace is free to everyone because God loves the world unconditionally. The only one who did pay the price for mankind's salvation is Jesus Christ. He willingly went to the Cross of Calvary and died for your sins and mine two thousand years ago. That's how much we mean to God, who painfully witnessed His own Son's pain, agony, suffering, and death on the Cross of Calvary. God demands righteousness from everyone and gives everything to us in return. God punishes everyone who rejects Him and His gift of salvation through His Son, Jesus Christ. **There's no way to avoid the inevitability of death and God's judgment.**

How many people have already died without making that critical decision to spend their eternity in heaven, instead, will burn eternally in the fires of hell? Making no decision is a decision for eternal damnation. So, make your decision right now for eternal salvation and not eternal condemnation! Choose life so when you take your last earthly breath, your next breath will be in the Kingdom of God. "And I saw thrones, and they sat upon them, and judgment was given unto them: and I saw the souls of them that were beheaded for the witness of Jesus, and for the word of God, and which had not worshipped the beast, neither his image, neither had received his mark upon their foreheads or in their hands; and they lived and reigned with Christ a thousand years" (Revelation 20:4 KJV).

Yes, those souls are alive in heaven because they made their decision for eternal life through Christ before they died and will reign with Him for one thousand years during the millennium. They were beheaded for their faith in Him and refused to take the Mark of the Beast, the Antichrist, on their forehead or hand. They reign with Jesus because they kept their faith in Him as their Savior until death.

What is the difference between the Judgment Seat of Christ and the White Throne Judgment? The Judgment Seat of Christ will evaluate the actions of every believer for rewards. Degrees of eternal rewards will be based on the deeds of the believer. The White Throne Judgment assesses all unbelievers' lives, who lived independently of the Lord and access their degree of punishments in the lake of fire.

No believer will face the White Throne Judgment because Christ was judged on the Cross of Calvary for their sins. He paid the price in full. Jesus guarantees eternal life for all believers who have faith in what He did on the cross for them. Believers only face the Judgment Seat of Christ for rewards, not our sins. Every sin committed from the moment we committed our first sin until our passing is paid in full by Jesus Christ. There is no condemnation for those who love God and accepts Jesus as their Lord and Savior!

We have all sinned and come short of the Glory of God. No one can make it into heaven on their own. Everyone needs our Savior, Jesus Christ. God so loved the world, He gave us His one and only Son as our Savior, so we don't have to die in our sins and take the same eternal punishment in hell originally prepared for the fallen angels. Everyone reading this book has to know, we all have free will to make that decision to either accept God's free amazing gift of salvation through His Son, Jesus, or refuse God's grace to blot out your sins. The non-believers will join Satan, the fallen angels, the false prophet, and the Antichrist in the fires of hell burning forever, where the flames are never quenched.

Chapter Summary

Jesus fulfilled what the prophets foretold of His first coming as the promised Jewish Messiah. Historical evidence points to the absolute truth with evidence beyond any reasonable doubt that Jesus Christ is the Son of God and the promised Jewish Messiah as prophesied in both the Old and New Testaments! In the Holy Bible, our messiah's virgin birth was attested to, His living a perfect and sinless life was attested to, dying on the Cross of Calvary as atonement for mankind's sins was documented and written by men divinely inspired by the Holy Spirit of God. His resurrection after three days was attested to, His remaining on earth for forty days was attested to, then ascending into heaven surrounded by heavenly angels with five hundred believers who witnessed His resurrection and ascension into heaven. Now Jesus sits in glory at the right hand of His Father. Every believer, alive or dead, knows He will soon return to rapture them into God's eternal kingdom, in their glorified resurrected bodies, where happiness and joy beyond our earthly comprehension await them!

The following Old and New Testament Scriptures confirm Christ's atonement for our sins.

Isaiah 53:4-6 NKJV

"Surely He has borne our griefs And carried our sorrows; Yet we esteemed Him stricken, Smitten by God, and afflicted. But He was wounded for our transgressions, He was bruised for our iniquities; The chastisement for our peace was upon Him, And by His stripes, we are healed. All we like sheep have gone astray;

We have turned, everyone, to his own way; And the Lord has laid on Him the iniquity of us all."

2 Corinthians 5:21 KJV
"For He hath made Him to be sin for us, who knew no sin; that we might be made the righteousness of God in Him."

1 Peter 2:24 NKJV
"Who Himself bore our sins in His own body on the tree, that we, having died to sins, might live for righteousness—by whose stripes you were healed."

Romans 3:24-26 ESV
"and are justified by His grace as a gift, through the redemption that is in Christ Jesus, whom God put forward as a propitiation by His blood, to be received by faith. This was to show God's righteousness because in His divine forbearance He had passed over former sins. It was to show His righteousness at the present time, so that He might be just and the justifier of the one who has faith in Jesus."

God's Holy Judgment requires a penalty of death as atonement for all sins. It was satisfied by His perfect and sinless Son. He was the only one who could qualify as our substitute because He was conceived without sin, and thereafter never committed any sin when He went to the Cross of Calvary. His death satisfied the demands of God's absolute holiness. Sin calls for judgment and Christ willingly paid the penalty for the sin of the world. "He is the atoning sacrifice for our sins, and not only for ours but also for the sins of the whole world" (1 John 2:2 NIV).

"Therefore, just as sin entered the world through one man, and death through sin, and in this way death came to all people because all sinned—To be sure, sin was in the world before the law was given, but sin is not charged against anyone's account where there is no law. Nevertheless, death reigned from the time of Adam to the time of Moses, even over those who did not sin by breaking a command, as did Adam, who is a pattern of the one to come. But the gift is not like the trespass. For if the many died by the trespass of the one man, how much more did God's grace and the gift that came by the grace of the one man, Jesus Christ, overflow to the many!" (Romans 5:12-15 NIV)

Every human being is under the curse of sin, whether one is immoral, moral, or religious. This curse of sin separates us from God and is inherited from our first parents, Adam and Eve. The only exception is the person of Jesus Christ who, through the virgin birth, escaped the sin problem that is normally passed down from generation to generation.

According to the Bible, Jesus's death on the cross satisfied God's wrath against sinful humanity:

"The wrath of God is being revealed from heaven against all the godlessness and wickedness of people, who suppress the truth by their wickedness since what may be known about God is plain to them because God has made it plain to them. For since the creation of the world God's invisible qualities—His eternal power and divine nature—have been clearly seen, being understood from what has been made, so that people are without excuse. For although they knew God, they neither glorified Him as God nor gave thanks to Him, but their thinking became futile and their foolish hearts were darkened. Although they claimed to be wise, they became fools and exchanged the glory of the immortal God for images made to look like a mortal human being and birds and animals and reptiles. Therefore God gave them over in the sinful desires of their hearts to sexual impurity for the degrading of their bodies with one another. They exchanged the truth about God for a lie and worshiped and served created things rather than the Creator—who is forever praised. Amen. Because of this, God gave them over to shameful lusts. Even their women exchanged natural sexual relations for unnatural ones. In the same way, the men also abandoned natural relations with women and were inflamed with lust for one another. Men committed shameful acts with other men and received in themselves the due penalty for their error. Furthermore, just as they did not think it worthwhile to retain the knowledge of God, so God gave them over to a depraved mind so that they do what ought not to be done. They have become filled with every kind of wickedness, evil, greed, and depravity. They are full of envy, murder, strife, deceit, and malice. They are gossips, slanderers, God-haters, insolent, arrogant, and boastful; they invent ways of doing evil; they disobey their parents; they have no understanding, no fidelity, no love, no mercy. Although they know God's righteous decree that those who do such things deserve death, they not only continue to do these very things but also approve of those who practice them" (Romans 1:18-32 NIV).

Time is of the essence for all to turn to the one and only Savior of humanity, Jesus Christ. REPENT AND LIVE!!!

CHAPTER TEN

The Holy Trinity:
God, Jesus, and the Holy Spirit

God is the sovereign ruler of the universe and is greater and more powerful than anything or anyone He ever created. He has no beginning and no end; He is the Alpha and the Omega. The Hebrew Scripture calls His name Yhwh. (pronounced "Yahweh") He is a Triune God in three distinct persons, God the Father, God the Son, and God the Holy Spirit. The three co-exist in three divine entities and are not independent of one another. God the Father directs each member of the Trinity to fulfill His will within the structure of His authority. As a Trinity, they always compliment each other and demonstrate God's Glory.

God the Father empowers the Son and the Holy Spirit to carry out His will. The Father sent His Son, Jesus, into the world as Savior and Redeemer. He's always obedient to God, the Father. In His farewell discourse, Jesus promised His disciples that upon His departure, He would send the Holy Spirit to them from the Father. To comfort them, lead them in all truth, remind them of the Words of Jesus, and empower them to carry out His commission to spread the Gospel. So as God sent Jesus to proclaim the Gospel to the world, Jesus sent His disciples to do the same.

Three times before His departure, Jesus asked Apostle Peter, brother of Andrew who led him to Jesus, "Do you love me?" "When they had finished breakfast, Jesus said to Simon Peter, 'Simon, do you love me more than these?' He said to Him, 'Yes, Lord; you know that I love you.' He said to him, 'Feed my lambs.' He said to him a second time, 'Simon, son of John, do you love me?' He said to Him, 'Yes, Lord; you know that I love you.' He said to him, 'Tend my sheep.' He said to him the third time, 'Simon, son of John, do you love me?' Peter was grieved because He said to him the third time, 'Do you love me?' and he said to Him, 'Lord, you know everything; you know that I love you.' Jesus said to him, 'Feed my sheep" (John 21:15-17 ESV).

That same commission, spoken to Peter three times, has been given to each one of us to spread the Gospel of Jesus Christ to the world. The Gospel message is that if we repent of our sins and make Jesus our Lord and Savior, all our sins are forgiven, and we are saved for all eternity and will dwell in the Kingdom of God forever.

The Biblical Doctrine of the Trinity of God is outlined in both the old and new testaments. From the beginning, God and the Holy Spirit always existed. Then, God created through His Holy Spirit, His only begotten Son, Jesus. Within the Trinity, all three are co-equal, co-eternal, and in complete unity with each other. They perform different functions. The Father is superior to the Son and the Holy Spirit. God is a spirit, the source, sender, and planner of all creation. After He created His Son, He created everything, including the angels and all mankind, through His only begotten Son, Jesus Christ. Jesus was created through the power of the third member of the Trinity, the Holy Spirit. Jesus, the second member of the Triune Godhead, said to His apostles, "You heard me say to you, 'I am going away, and I will come to you.'

If you loved me, you would have rejoiced, because I am going to the Father, for the Father is greater than I" (John 14:28 ESV).

Jesus is also called the Son of Man because He's fully God and fully man. As Son of Man, Jesus said, "Foxes have holes, and birds of the air have nests, but the Son of Man has nowhere to lay His head" (Matthew 8:20 ESV).

Jesus has a glorified heavenly body and sits at the right hand of God's Throne in Heaven. He is the achiever who always carries out the Will of the Father and keeps all His Commandments. God ordained Jesus to rule and reign over the entire universe and all the nations of the world.

To save mankind from eternal damnation in the fires of Hell, God appointed His Only Begotten Son, Jesus, to be the atonement for mankind's sin. To do this, His Son could not be born of a man, where the seed of sin passed from our first parents, Adam and Eve, to all their offspring. For the seed to be without the blemish of original sin, Jesus had to be born of a virgin, live a perfect life, and offer His life on the Cross of Calvary for God's forgiveness of mankind's sins. This was necessary to satisfy God's Judgment on mankind's sins. Jesus had to give His earthly life, as the Son of Mankind on the Cross of Calvary, to atone for every sin of the world.

"Carrying His own cross, He went out to the place of the Skull (which in Aramaic is called Golgotha). There they crucified Him and with Him two others—one on each side and Jesus in the middle. Pilate had a notice prepared and fastened to the cross. It read: Jesus of Nazareth, the king of the Jews. Many of the Jews read this sign, for the place where Jesus was crucified was near the city, and the sign was written in Aramaic, Latin, and Greek. The chief priests of the Jews protested to Pilate, 'Do not write 'The

King of the Jews, but that this man claimed to be king of the Jews.' Pilate answered, 'What I have written, I have written.' When the soldiers crucified Jesus, they took His clothes, dividing them into four shares, one for each of them, with the undergarment remaining. This garment was seamless, woven in one piece from top to bottom. 'Let's not tear it,' they said to one another. 'Let's decide by lot who will get it.' This happened that the scripture might be fulfilled that said, 'They divided my clothes among them and cast lots for my garment.' So this is what the soldiers did. Near the cross of Jesus stood His mother, His mother's sister, Mary the wife of Clopas, and Mary Magdalene. When Jesus saw His mother there, and the disciple whom He loved standing nearby, He said to her, 'Woman, here is your son,' and to the disciple, 'Here is your mother.' From that time on, this disciple took her into his home. Later, knowing that everything had now been finished, and so that Scripture would be fulfilled, Jesus said, 'I am thirsty.' A jar of wine vinegar was there, so they soaked a sponge in it, put the sponge on a stalk of the hyssop plant, and lifted it to Jesus' lips. When He had received the drink, Jesus said, 'It is finished.' With that, He bowed His head and gave up His spirit. Now it was the day of Preparation, and the next day was to be a special Sabbath. Because the Jewish leaders did not want the bodies left on the crosses during the Sabbath, they asked Pilate to have the legs broken and the bodies were taken down. The soldiers therefore came and broke the legs of the first man who had been crucified with Jesus, and then those of the other. But when they came to Jesus and found that He was already dead, they did not break His legs. Instead, one of the soldiers pierced Jesus' side with a spear, bringing a sudden flow of blood and water. The man who saw it has given testimony, and his testimony is true. He knows that he tells the truth, and he testifies so that you also may believe. These things happened so that the scripture would be fulfilled: 'Not one of His bones will be broken,' and, as another scripture says, 'They will look on the one they have pierced" (John 19:17-37 NIV).

How did the impregnation of Jesus without a man come about to a virgin girl named Mary? This was truly the only immaculate conception of any human being by God's Holy Spirit, who is the only one who can give life.

Mary was in her early teens and resided in the town of Nazareth in Galilee, most likely, with her parents. She knew no man but was betrothed to a man named Joeseph. Betrothal is the first stage of a Jewish marriage. One day when she was at the well for water, the angel Gabriel announced to her that she would be the mother of the promised Messiah by conceiving Him through the Holy Spirit.

"This is how the birth of Jesus the Messiah came about: His mother Mary was pledged to be married to Joseph, but before they came together, she was found to be pregnant through the Holy Spirit. Because Joseph her husband was faithful to the law, and yet did not want to expose her to public disgrace, he had in mind to divorce her quietly. But after he had considered this, an angel of the Lord appeared to him in a dream and said, 'Joseph son of David, do not be afraid to take Mary home as your wife, because what is conceived in her is from the Holy Spirit. She will give birth to a son, and you are to give Him the name Jesus because He will save His people from their sins.' All this took place to fulfill what the Lord had said through the prophet: 'The virgin will conceive and give birth to a son, and they will call Him Immanuel' (which means 'God with us'). When Joseph woke up, he did what the angel of the Lord had commanded him and took

Mary home as his wife. But he did not consummate their marriage until she gave birth to a son. And he gave Him the name Jesus" (Matthew 1:18-25 NIV).

The function of the Holy Spirit is to be in subordination to the will of the Father. This means the Father sends the Holy Spirit to fulfill His assignments. The Holy Spirit does not send the Father, nor does the Son send the Father. The Father is the only one who sends both. In summary, God the Father is the planner. God the Son is the executor of God's plans, and God, the Holy Spirit, is the one who accomplishes the will of the Father. All pray to God, the Father, in the name of Jesus, through the Holy Spirit. "In that day you will no longer ask me anything. Very truly I tell you, my Father will give you whatever you ask in my name" (John 16:23 NIV).

In Genesis 1:26-27, "Then God said, 'Let us make mankind in our image, in our likeness, so that they may rule over the fish in the sea and the birds in the sky, over the livestock and all the wild animals, and over all the creatures that move along the ground. So God created mankind in His own image, in the image of God He created them; male and female He created them." (NIV)

Chapter Summary

We have one God in three persons. Who are all equally omniscient, omnipotent, omnipresent, eternal, and unchanging, each having their unique functions. The Holy Spirit was present with God from the beginning before God created His only Son, Jesus Christ. God created all things through Him that were made, and nothing was made without Him. God designed how mankind would be redeemed in the Garden of Eden. He ordained His only begotten Son to accomplish His will to save mankind through

His life and death on the cross. The Holy Spirit sees to it that every person receives the call for God's saving grace. Mankind can be forgiven for every sin committed. "But if we walk in the light, as He is in the light, we have fellowship with one another, and the blood of Jesus, His Son, purifies us from all sin" (1 John 1:7 NIV).

CHAPTER ELEVEN

Old Testament Prophet's Account of the Jewish Messiah

The Old Testament Prophets did not mention Jesus by His name. However, Moses, who wrote the first five books of the Bible, called the Torah, to other prophets, such as Jeremiah, Micah, Zechariah, and Lehi wrote about the Jewish Messiah's life. King David wrote Psalm 22, describing the crucifixion of the Jewish Messiah a thousand years before the birth of Jesus. Isaiah Chapter 53:1-12 was written seven hundred years before the first coming of the Jewish Messiah and gave a full account of His life and His crucifixion on the cross. Isaiah is the only prophet that God revealed the creation of the New Heaven and the New Earth beyond the thousand-year millennium. The Old Testament Prophets' accounts' lined up with the first coming of Jesus

King David outlined word-for-word what Jesus Christ, the Jewish Messiah, would say as His hands and feet were nailed to the cross for the sins of the world. He willingly gave up His life to atone for everyone's sins. All who repent of their sins and accept Jesus Christ as their Lord and Savior will be washed clean from every sin they ever committed, past, present, and future, and will inherit the Kingdom of God forever. Once we accept

Jesus as our Lord and Savior, we are under grace, not the law. "Therefore, there is now no condemnation for those who are in Christ Jesus" (Romans 8:1 NIV).

Psalm 22 (NKJV)

[1] My God, My God, why have You forsaken Me?

Why are You so far from helping Me,

And from the words of My groaning?

[2] O My God, I cry in the daytime, but You do not hear;

And in the night season, and am not silent.

[3] But You are holy,

Enthroned in the praises of Israel.

[4] Our fathers trusted in You;

They trusted, and You delivered them.

[5] They cried to You, and were delivered;

They trusted in You and were not ashamed.

[6] But I am a worm, and no man;

A reproach of men, and despised by the people.

[7] All those who see Me ridicule Me;

They shoot out the lip, they shake the head, saying,

[8] He trusted in the Lord, let Him rescue Him;

Let Him deliver Him since He delights in Him!

[9] But You are He who took Me out of the womb;

You made Me trust while on My mother's breasts.

[10] I was cast upon You from birth.

From My mother's womb

You have been My God.

[11] Be not far from Me,

For trouble is near;

For there is none to help.

[12] Many bulls have surrounded Me;

Strong bulls of Bashan have encircled Me.

[13] They gape at Me with their mouths,

Like a raging and roaring lion.

[14] I am poured out like water,

And all My bones are out of joint;

My heart is like wax;

It has melted within Me.

[15] My strength is dried up like a potsherd,

And My tongue clings to My jaws;

You have brought Me to the dust of death.

[16] For dogs have surrounded Me;

The congregation of the wicked has enclosed Me.

They pierced My hands and My feet;

[17] I can count all My bones.

They look and stare at Me.

[18] They divide My garments among them,

And for My clothing they cast lots.

[19] But You, O Lord, do not be far from Me;

O My Strength, hasten to help Me!

[20] Deliver Me from the sword,

My precious life from the power of the dog.

[21] Save Me from the lion's mouth

And from the horns of the wild oxen!

You have answered Me.

[22] I will declare Your name to My brethren;

In the midst of the assembly, I will praise You.

[23] You who fear the Lord, praise Him!

All you descendants of Jacob, glorify Him,

And fear Him, all you offspring of Israel!

[24] For He has not despised nor abhorred the affliction of the afflicted;

Nor has He hidden His face from Him;

But when He cried to Him, He heard.

[25] My praise shall be of You in the great assembly;

I will pay My vows before those who fear Him.

[26] The poor shall eat and be satisfied;

Those who seek Him will praise the Lord.

Let your heart live forever!

[27] All the ends of the world

Shall remember and turn to the Lord,

And all the families of the nations

Shall worship before You.

[28] For the kingdom is the Lord's,

And He rules over the nations.

[29] All the prosperous of the earth

Shall eat and worship;

All those who go down to the dust

Shall bow before Him,

Even he who cannot keep himself alive.

[30] A posterity shall serve Him.

It will be recounted of the Lord to the next generation,

[31] They will come and declare His righteousness to a people who will be born,

That He has done this.

The Prophet Isaiah described the Bible story of the life of Jesus seven hundred years before His birth.

Isaiah 53 (NKJV)

1. Who has believed our report?

And to whom has the arm of the Lord been revealed?

2. For He shall grow up before Him as a tender plant,

And as a root out of the dry ground.

He has no form or comeliness;

And when we see Him,

There is no beauty that we should desire Him.

3. He is despised and rejected by men,

A Man of sorrows and acquainted with grief.

And we hid, as it were, our faces from Him;

He was despised, and we did not esteem Him.

4. Surely He has borne our griefs

And carried our sorrows;

Yet we esteemed Him stricken,

Smitten by God, and afflicted.

5. But He was wounded for our transgressions,

He was bruised for our iniquities;

The chastisement for our peace was upon Him,

And by His stripes, we are healed.

6. All we like sheep have gone astray;

We have turned, everyone, to his own way;

And the Lord has laid on Him the iniquity of us all.

7. He was oppressed and He was afflicted,

Yet He opened not His mouth;

He was led as a lamb to the slaughter,

And as a sheep before its shearers is silent,

So He opened not His mouth.

8. He was taken from prison and from judgment,

And who will declare His generation?

For He was cut off from the land of the living;

For the transgressions of My people, He was stricken.

9. And they made His grave with the wicked —

But with the rich at His death,

Because He had done no violence,

Nor was any deceit in His mouth.

10. Yet it pleased the Lord to bruise Him;

He has put Him to grief.

When You make His soul an offering for sin,

He shall see His seed, He shall prolong His days,

And the pleasure of the Lord shall prosper in His hand.

11. He shall see the labor of His soul, and be satisfied.

By His knowledge, My righteous Servant shall justify many,

For He shall bear their iniquities.

12. Therefore I will divide Him a portion with the great,

And He shall divide the [s]spoil with the strong,

Because He poured out His soul unto death,

And He was numbered with the transgressors,

And He bore the sin of many,

And made intercession for the transgressors.

These Scriptures, written by the Old Testament Prophets, are accurate accounts of the Jewish Messiah's birth, life, and death. Both in the Bible and other historical literature, it is well documented that Jesus is the Jewish Messiah that fulfilled Bible Prophesy with His coming to earth two thousand years ago. There is infallible historical evidence that Jesus was given birth by a young virgin girl named Mary, and His earthly father was Joseph. He grew up with brothers and sisters and worked with His father as a carpenter. It's also well documented that He went to the Jordan River to be baptized by His cousin, John, who was called the Baptist because he was the forerunner, baptizing people until the Messiah would appear. John saw a man come to the river to be baptized and immediately knew this was the Messiah. He, along with witnesses, saw and heard the following account of the Jewish Messiah in The Gospel of Matthew.

"In those days John the Baptist came preaching in the wilderness of Judea, and saying, 'Repent, for the kingdom of heaven is at hand!' For this is he who was spoken of by the prophet Isaiah, saying: 'The voice of one crying in the wilderness: 'Prepare the way of the Lord; Make His paths straight.'' Now John himself was clothed in camel's hair, with a leather belt around his waist; and his food was locusts and wild honey. Then Jerusalem, all Judea, and all the region around the Jordan went out to him and were baptized by him in the Jordan, confessing their sins. But when he saw many of the Pharisees and Sadducees coming to his baptism, he said to them, 'Brood of vipers! Who warned you to flee from the wrath to come? Therefore bear fruits worthy of repentance, and do not think to say to yourselves, 'We have Abraham as our father.' For I say to you that God is able to raise up children to Abraham from these stones. And even now the ax is laid to the root of the trees. Therefore every tree which does not bear good fruit is cut down and thrown into the fire. I indeed baptize you with water unto repentance, but He who is coming after me is mightier than I, whose sandals I am not worthy to carry. He will baptize you with the Holy Spirit and fire. His winnowing fan is in His hand, and He will thoroughly clean out His threshing floor, and gather His wheat into the barn, but He will burn up the chaff with unquenchable fire.' Then Jesus came from Galilee to John at the Jordan to be baptized by him. And John tried to prevent Him, saying, 'I need to be baptized by You, and are You coming to me?' But Jesus answered and said to him, 'Permit it to be so now, for thus it is fitting for us to fulfill all righteousness.' Then he allowed Him. When He had been baptized, Jesus came up immediately from the water; and behold, the heavens were opened to Him, and He saw the Spirit of God descending like a dove and alighting upon Him. And suddenly a voice came from heaven, saying, 'This is My beloved Son, in whom I am well pleased" (Matthew 3 NKJV).

When God audibly spoke from Heaven and said, "This is My beloved Son, in whom I am well pleased," it became indisputable proof that Jesus is truly the Son of God.

During Jesus's three and a half years of ministry, He traveled on foot to preach the Good News of His Father's Gospel of Eternal Life for everyone who would repent of their sins and accept His Son, Jesus, as atonement for their sins. Today, in 2021, the final prophetic signs are proliferating throughout the world, signaling His Second Coming. Jesus warned that fools (non-believers) would see these signs and pass on, but the wise (believers) will see the signs and know their redemption from this Satanic world is imminent!

Jesus is coming soon, and everyone who by faith believes in Him and repents of their sins will be raptured from this earth into the Kingdom of God. There, we will live forever and have a glorious life. The Bible says there are no words to describe what God has in store for all those who love Him because it will be so incredibly awesome!

The Bible and historical records attest that the Jewish Messiah is Jesus Christ, the Son of God. His birth, life, death on the cross, resurrection, and ascension to Heaven is recorded in history and the Bible. Those who choose not to believe in Him will be judged at the White Throne Judgment, and everyone that is not found in the Lamb's (Jesus) Book of Life will be thrust into the fires of Hell, where the flames and worms will be eternal.

CHAPTER TWELVE

The Crucifixion
of Jesus Christ

Jesus Christ, the Son of God, is fully God and fully man. He willingly underwent unbearable and horrific pain and suffering to atone for the sins of humanity. He allowed His body to be sacrificed on a wooden cross with only a garment covering His private manhood. His hands and feet were brutally and harshly nailed to a wooden cross. He bore pain and suffering while being publicly tortured and punished for telling the truth that He was the Son of God. A crown of thorns was cruelly pushed into His scalp and forehead while blood poured down His already beaten and bloody face. There wasn't a place on His entire body that wasn't beaten, whipped, or tortured. Roman soldiers beat His body thirty-nine times with a lead-tipped whip called a flagrum. The purpose of the Roman flagrum was to beat a person to the point of death. It pulled the flesh from the body.

The Shroud of Turin is the most intensely investigated religious artifact in all of world history, which shows the horrendous wounds of a crucified man, with wounds exactly matching the description of Jesus's crucifixion wounds. Many scholars believe it may be the linen cloth He was buried in that was wrapped around His body. With the possibility that at the moment of His resurrection, radiation could have emanated from His body, leaving on the shroud the marks of Jesus's scourging and crucifixion wounds.

Jesus was spat on, mocked, and the crowd yelled out false accusations while He willingly carried the heavy cross through the streets of the Via Dolorosa (Latin for sorrowful way), a processional route that the Roman soldiers forced Jesus to walk on the way to His crucifixion. The crowd never let up on their heckling and yelling profanities as He went to His execution on the cross. He bore all this for the sins of mankind, who He created out of love.

Jesus stayed alive on the cross for several torturous hours, during which time He spoke these final seven words:

"Father, forgive them, for they know not what they do" (Luke 23:34 KJV).

Jesus gave us an important example of forgiving and praying. After all Jesus was put through from being painfully nailed to the cross, His only thought was of saving mankind. From the time of the Creation, the salvation of mankind was His main and most important goal. He wants us to be soul winners as well.

"Those who are wise will shine like the brightness of the heavens, and those who lead many to righteousness, like the stars forever and ever" (Daniel 12:3 NIV).

"Today, you will be with me in paradise" (Luke 23:43 KJV).

Jesus promised this to the thief on the cross on His right side, who asked, "Jesus, remember me when you come into your kingdom" (Luke 23:42 NIV). There was also a thief on the cross to His left side who mocked Him and said, "Aren't you the Messiah? Save yourself and us!" (Luke 23:39 NIV) Here we witness a believer on His right side who Jesus promised would be with Him that same day in God's Kingdom, and a non-believer who would die in his own sins. In the Holy Scriptures, there is insurmountable evidence that God promises mankind eternal salvation through faith in His Son and not a religion or good works. The disbelieving thief on Jesus's left side was not saved, but the thief on the right side, through faith, was. "For it is by grace you have been saved, through faith—and this is not from yourselves, it is the gift of God—not by works, so that no one can boast" (Ephesians 2:8-9 NIV).

"Woman here is your son" (John 19:26 NIV) and to John, His beloved Apostle,

"Here is your mother" (John 19:27 NIV).

Despite His excruciating physical agony, Jesus was concerned about the welfare of His mother and the pain she was experiencing. With His thoughts on Mary's future security and protection, Jesus entrusted her into the care of John, His beloved disciple. Jesus most likely chose John out of profound spiritual concern for His mother. Even in death, Christ was focused on spiritual matters.

"My God, my God, why have you forsaken me?" (Matthew 27:46 NIV)

To many, this is the most surprising Scripture in the whole Bible! Jesus spoke those words at the height of His agony. Many believe that God turned away for only a brief moment because He suffered seeing the torture of His only Son, being beaten, mocked, spit on, whipped, pierced with a crown of thorns on His head, and nailed to a cross. It was heart-wrenching for God to watch His Son hang there for several hours on the cross while He was in sheer agony. This was the most difficult, painful moment of God's entire existence to witness His own Son's agony on the cross. Our Heavenly Father feels that way about every one of us. He takes no pleasure in our suffering or death. "For I take no pleasure in the death of anyone, declares the Sovereign Lord. Repent and live!" (Ezekiel 18:32 NIV)

"I am thirsty" (John 19:28 NIV)

In His final moments on the Cross, Jesus submitted himself to very human, vulnerable feelings of emptiness and need both in body and spirit. He allows Himself to be brought to the pit of all thirst. He feels bodily thirst as He's pushed to His limits near death. But, He is also thirsting for souls. His thirst is a burning desire to give! His thirst is a desire to pour out love and mercy.

"It is finished" (John 19:30 NIV).

This statement from Jesus while on the cross is one that every believer can stand on for confidence in their walk with God. These may be the most powerful words ever spoken! Jesus bore the sentence of all of our sins. The price for every mistake and transgression was completely paid in full. He fulfilled the law and destroyed the works of the devil once and for all. "It is finished" is more than a saying; it is a battle cry of victory for every Christian. The wages of sin may be death, but with the sacrifice of Jesus' life on the cross, we have life and have it in abundance! We no longer need to fear death.

"Father, into your hands I commit my spirit" (Luke 23:46 NIV).

Jesus died on 14 Nisan, 3793 Anno Mundi— Friday, April 3, AD 33 at about 3 p.m., a few hours before the beginning of Passover and the Sabbath. With Jesus's last breath came a great earthquake. The veil in the temple tore completely in half. Those around Him saw what He had done along with the signs that followed and were amazed. The Gospels point to the Roman guard who made a bold statement at the foot of the cross. "Surely He was the Son of God!" (Matthew 27:54 NIV) The same guards that were mocking, abusing Him, and gambling for His clothes were now expressing words of praise.

Pray now to accept Jesus Christ as your Savior:

Dear God,

I know that I'm a sinner and that nothing I do can gain me eternal life in Heaven. I repent of all my sins, past, present, and future. I believe your Son; Jesus Christ died for me and rose from the grave. Right now, I receive Him as my Lord and Savior by trusting in Him alone as my only way to Heaven. Thank you for giving me eternal life through faith in Your Son. Amen.

____

Sign your name as a believer in Jesus.

"If you declare with your mouth, "Jesus is Lord," and believe in your heart that God raised Him from the dead, you will be saved. For it is with your heart that you believe and are justified, and it is with your mouth that you profess your faith and are saved" (Romans 10:9-10 NIV).

"Whoever believes in Him is not condemned, but whoever does not believe stands condemned already because they have not believed in the name of God's one and only Son" (John 3:18 NIV).

CHAPTER THIRTEEN

The Holy Spirit Dwells Within
Every Believer Eternally

The Holy Spirit is the third member of the Holy Trinity and the inspirational author of the sixty-six books of the Bible. "For prophecy never had its origin in the human will, but prophets, though human, spoke from God as they were carried along by the Holy Spirit" (2 Peter 1:21 NIV). His attributes include wisdom, understanding, counsel, fortitude, knowledge, piety, and fear of the Lord. He gives divine intervention to fulfill one's destiny and is a comforter, counselor, and advocate for every believer, respectively. He bears witness they belong to God, and very importantly, assures them of their eternal salvation through Jesus Christ. The Bible teaches that the Holy Spirit is active in our lives and is a distinct person and fully God, who speaks to our spiritual being. He doesn't have a physical body like Jesus but is a person who lived eternally with God the Father, who is a spirit, and God the Son.

To every believer, the Holy Spirit dispenses at will His gifts, which are: words of wisdom, words of knowledge, the gift of faith, the gift of healing, working of miracles, prophecy, discernment between good and evil spirits, and speaking in tongues. The

Holy Spirit is a person with feelings and has a mind, a will, and emotions. He wants to fellowship with every believer. Apostle Paul wrote in his second letter to the Corinthians, "May the grace of the Lord Jesus Christ, and the love of God, and the fellowship of the Holy Spirit be with you all" (2 Corinthians 13:14 NIV). The Holy Spirit can have fellowship and communion with us. In every sense of the word, He is a real person, like Jesus is a person, and God is a spiritual being. The Holy Spirit can pray for us just as Jesus is praying for us now. He teaches us what we need to know to live a good life. He guides and directs us in making the right decisions. He is all-knowing, all-seeing, and is everywhere while always being present with God. The words of God are the words of the Holy Spirit. We are the Temple of God because the Holy Spirit dwells within us.

When Jesus was baptized in the Jordan River by His cousin, John the Baptist, the Holy Spirit appeared as a dove and rested upon Him. All three members of the Holy Trinity were present simultaneously and are distinct from one another. The Holy Spirit has lived with the Father and the Son since before the beginning of time. God created us to live in their loving and close relationship. They enjoy fellowship with each other and want us to enjoy fellowship with them.

The Holy Spirit can not dwell in a non-believer, only within every believer. He never leaves us and always works to inspire us to fulfill our destiny set before us by God. He convicts the world of sin and regenerates the repentant believer. He gives us the blessed assurance that we are saved through Jesus. He wills for us to live a righteous life. He is always present and sanctifies each of us with the power to live a Holy life and to be a witness for God. He gives us discernment of the Holy Scriptures. He enables us to exhibit the Fruits of the Spirit, which are love, joy, peace, patience, kindness, generosity, faithfulness, gentleness, and self-control. Using these gifts, He leads us to bear much fruit and success in our life.

He is that voice in our spirit who talks to us. He was active in creation and inspired the forty writers of the Holy Scriptures. He convicts the world of sin, guaranteeing our inheritance in heaven, and seals us for the day of redemption. He teaches us that the only way to salvation is through God's only begotten Son, Jesus Christ.

To fulfill God's Son as an atonement for mankind's sins, the Holy Spirit placed the seed of the Son of God, Jesus Christ, in the womb of a young teenage virgin named Mary. Jesus was born in the little town of Bethlehem. He grew up in strength and wisdom. He lived a perfect life without any blemish of sin and then took upon Himself the ultimate punishment of God's judgment, death, and damnation. He did this by dying on the Cross of Calvary for the sins of humanity. "For God so loved the world that He gave His one and only son, that whoever believes in Him shall not perish but have eternal life" (John 3:16 NIV).

All we have to do to receive forgiveness and be exonerated from all our sins is to repent of our sins and make Jesus the Lord and Savior of our life. By doing this, we are redeemed from all our sins and inherit eternal life in God's Kingdom, and have the indwelling of the Holy Spirit forever. Jesus promised His apostles, before His death by crucifixion, that after He left them, He would ask His Father to send the Comforter, the Holy Spirit, to them. "And I will ask the Father, and He will give you another advocate to help you and be with you forever—the Spirit of truth. The world cannot accept Him, because it neither sees Him nor knows Him. But you know Him, for He lives with you and will be in you" (John 14:16-17 NIV).

Christ's death on the cross not only paid all of mankind's sins in full but included the original sin of our first parents, Adam and Eve. **The only sin that is not forgiven in this life or the next is when we blaspheme the Holy Spirit.** We commit this unforgivable sin against the Holy Spirit by refusing to accept Jesus's sacrifice on the cross as an atonement for our sins. "And everyone who speaks a word against the Son of Man will be forgiven, but anyone who blasphemes against the Holy Spirit will not be forgiven" (Luke 12:10 NIV).

The power of Jesus' resurrection assures every repentant sinner of a second chance. Our Heavenly Father is not only the God of second chances but countless chances. His forgiveness is irrevocable for those who repented of their sins and accepted His Son, Jesus, as their Savior.

Jesus states, "I am the way and the truth and the life. No one comes to the Father except through me." (John 14:6 NIV). The Holy Spirit confirms this in countless Scriptures throughout the Holy Bible that the only way to salvation is through the Son of God. Yet those who take their last breath without accepting God's free gift of salvation through His Son Jesus Christ end all opportunity to be forgiven for their sins. If anyone, regardless of their religious beliefs, does not accept Jesus, they must face God at the White Throne Judgment and take full responsibility and punishment for their sins, which is unbearable pain and suffering in the eternal fires of Hell.

The only life ahead for the non-believer is the eternal torment of hellfire with unquenchable flames that will encircle them forever!

On the other side of eternity, just the opposite is waiting for every believer in Jesus Christ. They will reside forever in God's Kingdom and possess His eternal love, joy, peace, and have the Blessed Assurance their joy will last forever.

These Holy Scriptures describe the punishments of Hell for all non-believers who die in their own sins:

Matthew 13:49-50 ESV
"So it will be at the end of the age. The angels will come out and separate the evil from the righteous and throw them into the fiery furnace. In that place, there will be weeping and gnashing of teeth."

Matthew 18:8 ESV
"And if your hand or your foot causes you to sin, cut it off and throw it away. It is better for you to enter life crippled or lame than with two hands or two feet to be thrown into the eternal fire."

Matthew 18:9 ESV
"And if your eye causes you to sin, tear it out and throw it away. It is better for you to enter life with one eye than with two eyes to be thrown into the hell of fire."

Matthew 25:41 ESV
"Then He will say to those on His left, 'Depart from me, you cursed, into the eternal fire prepared for the devil and his angels.'"

Revelation 19:20 ESV
"And the beast was captured, and with it the false prophet who in its presence had done the signs by which he deceived those who had received the mark of the beast and those who worshiped its image. These two were thrown alive into the lake of fire that burns with sulfur."

Revelation 20:10 ESV
"And the devil who had deceived them was thrown into the lake of fire and sulfur where the beast and the false prophet were, and they will be tormented day and night forever and ever."

Revelation 20:14-15 ESV
"Then death and hades were thrown into the lake of fire. This is the second death, the lake of fire. And if anyone's name was not found written in the book of life, he was thrown into the lake of fire."

Revelation 21:8 ESV
"But as for the cowardly, the faithless, the detestable, as for murderers, the sexually immoral, sorcerers, idolaters, and all liars, their portion will be in the lake that burns with fire and sulfur, which is the second death."

Revelation 14:10 ESV
"He also will drink the wine of God's wrath, poured full strength into the cup of his anger, and he will be tormented with fire and sulfur in the presence of the holy angels and in the presence of the Lamb."

CHAPTER FOURTEEN

Lucifer Cast Out of Heaven Down to Earth

God created Lucifer as a guardian cherub who was given very special attributes. He had the high position of hovering over and protecting the very Throne of God on His Holy Mountain. Lucifer was blameless from the beginning of his creation until his pride and vanity caused him to deeply covet God's Throne and all the worship he received from the angels. He thought he could successfully take over God's entire Kingdom for himself. His conceit clouded all logic that he would lose the battle and inherit God's eternal judgment.

All he could think of was being worshiped by all the angels and being as God. Lucifer did not acknowledge that it was God who created him and gave him all his powers. Instead of being satisfied with all that God gave him, he became so impressed with his own beauty, intelligence, power, and position that he began to desire for himself the honor and glory that belongs only to God alone. This pride represents the actual beginning of sin in the universe—preceding the fall of our first parents, Adam and Eve. Nevertheless, being determined in his quest to remove God from His throne, he convinced one-third of God's angels to follow him in his heavenly rebellion. Without thinking of any consequences, Lucifer started the heavenly coup d'etat (coup) against God.

"Then war broke out in heaven. Michael and his angels fought against the dragon, and the dragon and his angels fought back. But he (Lucifer)was not strong enough, and they lost their place in heaven. **The great dragon was hurled down that ancient serpent called the devil, or Satan, who leads the whole world astray. He was hurled to the earth and his angels with him.** Then I heard a loud voice in heaven say: "Now have come the salvation and the power and the kingdom of our God, and the authority of His Messiah. For the accuser of our brothers and sisters, who accuses them before our God day and night, has been hurled down. They triumphed over him by the blood of the Lamb and by the word of their testimony; they did not love their lives so much as to shrink from death. Therefore rejoice, you heavens and you who dwell in them! But woe to the earth and the sea, because the devil has gone down to you! He is filled with fury because he knows that his time is short." (Revelation 12:7-12 NIV).

Satan was defeated by Michael, the archangel, and his angels and thrown down to earth. He and the fallen angels lost their heavenly positions, but God allowed Satan to keep his power, which he uses for evil continually.

Lucifer's war in heaven against God for supremacy is detailed in two Old Testament chapters:

Ezekiel 28:11-19 (NIV)
"The word of the Lord came to me: "Son of man, take up a lament concerning the king of Tyre and say to him: 'This is what the Sovereign Lord says: "You were the seal of perfection, full of wisdom

and perfect in beauty. You were in Eden, the garden of God; every precious stone adorned you: carnelian, chrysolite, and emerald, topaz, onyx and jasper, lapis lazuli, turquoise, and beryl. Your settings and mountings were made of gold; on the day you were created they were prepared. You were anointed as a guardian cherub, for so I ordained you. You were on the holy mount of God; you walked among the fiery stones. You were blameless in your ways from the day you were created till wickedness was found in you. Through your widespread trade, you were filled with violence, and you sinned. So, I drove you in disgrace from the mount of God, and I expelled you, guardian cherub, from among the fiery stones. Your heart became proud on account of your beauty, and you corrupted your wisdom because of your splendor. So, I threw you to the earth; I made a spectacle of you before kings. By your many sins and dishonest trade, you have desecrated your sanctuaries. So, I made a fire come out from you, and it consumed you and I reduced you to ashes on the ground in the sight of all who were watching. All the nations who knew you are appalled at you; you have come to a horrible end and will be no more." (NOTE: 1 Timothy 3:6 also refers to Satan's conceit)

Isaiah 14:12-14 (NKJV)

"How you are fallen from heaven, O Lucifer, son of the morning! How you are cut down to the ground, you who weakened the nations! For you have said in your heart: 'I will ascend into heaven, I will exalt my throne above the stars of God; I will also sit on the mount of the congregation on the farthest sides of the north; I will ascend above the heights of the clouds, I will be like the High.'" (Satan says five times, "I will," which shows his superabundance of pride and vanity.)

Satan on Earth

Since losing his high heavenly position and being thrown down to earth with his fallen angels, the Bible confirms they are on earth, causing countless problems and havoc in everyone's life. After the fall, God changed Lucifer's name from "Morning Star" to Satan, "adversary." At the Second Coming of Jesus Christ, which is imminent, Satan will be defeated and bound in the bottomless pit during Christ's thousand-year millennial kingdom. After the thousand years are up, Satan will be let loose for a little while to deceive the nations again to war against the elect. "And cast him into the bottomless pit, and shut him up, and set a seal upon him, that he should deceive the nations no more, till the thousand years should be fulfilled: and after that, he must be loosed a little season" (Revelation 20:3 KJV).

Our world is witnessing the effects of Satan's rulership, with his demons, who are imploding our world with countless upheavals which are causing serious problems. This includes moral wickedness, depravity, corruption, pain, misery, and creating one disaster after another for our planet. One troubling issue now facing our country and the entire world is a nuclear conflagration with foreign leaders like Iran, China, Russia, Turkey, and other nations who are ready and able to go to war at any time. Signs of this happening are all around us. According to Bible prophecy, these events will occur during these final days just before Jesus' 2nd coming. Are we ready? Is our current President, Joseph Robinette Biden, ready? Are our government and our political leaders prepared to deal with these major events that would include World War III with the probability of a nuclear war and threat of cyber-warfare? These are real possibilities facing our nation today that are provoking thoughts of fear, confusion, and trepidations, especially among our political leaders.

Daily, there's breaking news of one upheaval after another with no apparent let-up. Families and societies worldwide are being affected by the dissensions worldwide. Satan's wrath is being poured out without measure while sowing turmoil in everyone's life. In one way or another, everyone is experiencing disruptions in their life. Globally, this includes the deadly COVID-19 virus and other variant pandemics that are now surfacing. There are violent storms, floods, hurricanes, tornadoes, which are destroying lives and infrastructure across the globe. Murder is running rampant. City riots are becoming more violent and deadly with a cry against racial discrimination, police brutality, and countless heinous crimes against the minority. These are real events breaking out worldwide and are adversely affecting everyone.

The family unit is being challenged with health and financial issues. Death tolls rise from plagues, and natural disasters, with calamities rising without any let-up. Will conditions ever get better? The Bible tells us it will only get worse. Matthew 24 is one of the most eye-opening chapters in the Bible that describes the chaos facing our world today. These signs show us we are truly living at the end of days.

In the beginning, God gave His first created man, Adam, possession of the planet earth and allowed him to have dominion over all the creatures and create kingdoms on earth. When Adam and Eve sinned by giving in to Satan's temptation, instead of obeying God, they lost their authority over planet earth and were cast out of the Garden of Eden. (See John 8:34, Romans 6:16, and Luke 4:4-8) Their disobedience handed possession of the planet over to their deceiver, Satan, the devil. He only uses his powers on earth for evil and to steal, kill and destroy. "The thief cometh not, but for to steal, and to kill, and to destroy: I have come that they might have life and that they might have it more abundantly" (John 10:10 KJV). With no exception, Satan is out to destroy everyone, regardless of race, color, or creed. He has authority over the fallen angels who work to assist him in his plan to destroy humanity completely. Today, we can see all the calamities and the effects they have caused in everyone's life: diseases, poverty, strife, pain, sorrow, and death. However, God is more powerful and has full ownership with control over planet earth and the entire universe. He only allows Satan to temporarily have authority and be ruler and "god" of this world until He destroys him from among the nations. (See John 8:34, Romans 6:16, and Luke 4:4-8). The Good News is that, as believers in Jesus Christ, we have the authority to cast out Satan from our life. We can do this just by proclaiming the name of Jesus, then Satan and his demons will flee from us.

The Bible tells us to put on the full armor of God against Satan and all his demons:
"Finally, be strong in the Lord and in His mighty power. Put on the full armor of God, so that you can take your stand against the devil's schemes. For our struggle is not against flesh and blood, but against the rulers, against the authorities, against the powers of this dark world, and the spiritual forces of evil in the heavenly realms. Therefore put on the full armor of God, so that when the day of evil comes, you may be able to stand your ground, and after you have done everything, to stand. Stand firm then, with the belt of truth buckled around your waist, with the breastplate of righteousness in place, and with your feet fitted with the readiness that comes from the gospel of peace. In addition to all this, take up the shield of faith, with which you can extinguish all the

flaming arrows of the evil one. Take the helmet of salvation and the sword of the Spirit, which is the word of God. And pray in the Spirit on all occasions with all kinds of prayers and requests. With this in mind, be alert and always keep on praying for all the Lord's people" (Ephesians 6:10-18 NIV).

Bible verses on Jesus's authority to cast out demons:

James 4:7 ESV
"Submit yourselves therefore to God. Resist the devil, and he will flee from you."

Mark 16:16-18 ESV
"Whoever believes and is baptized will be saved, but whoever does not believe will be condemned. And these signs will accompany those who believe: in my name, they will cast out demons; they will speak in new tongues; they will pick up serpents with their hands; and if they drink any deadly poison, it will not hurt them; they will lay their hands on the sick, and they will recover."

Luke 10:17 ESV
"The seventy-two returned with joy, saying, 'Lord, even the demons are subject to us in your name!'"

Mark 3:11 ESV
"And whenever the unclean spirits saw Him, they fell down before Him and cried out, 'you are the Son of God.'"

Mark 9:29 ESV
"And He said to them, 'this kind cannot be driven out by anything but prayer.'"

Acts 16:16-18 ESV
"As we were going to the place of prayer, we were met by a slave girl who had a spirit of divination and brought her owners much gain by fortune-telling. She followed Paul and us, crying out,

'These men are servants of the Most High God, who proclaim to you the way of salvation.' And this she kept doing for many days. Paul, having become greatly annoyed, turned and said to the spirit, 'I command you in the name of Jesus Christ to come out of her." And it came out that very hour.'"

1 John 4:1-3 ESV

"Beloved, do not believe every spirit but test the spirits to see whether they are from God, for many false prophets have gone out into the world. By this you know the spirit of God: every spirit that confesses that Jesus Christ has come in the flesh is from God, and every spirit that does not confess Jesus is not from god. This is the spirit of the antichrist, which you heard was coming and now is in the world already."

Luke 4:33-36 ESV

"And in the synagogue, there was a man who had the spirit of an unclean demon, and he cried out with a loud voice, 'Ha! What have you to do with us, Jesus of Nazareth? Have you come to destroy us? I know who you are— the Holy One of God.' But Jesus rebuked him, saying, 'Be silent and come out of him!' And when the demon had thrown him down in their midst, he came out of him, having done him no harm. And they were all amazed and said to one another, 'What is this word? For with authority and power, He commands the unclean spirits, and they come out!'"

John 14:11-13 ESV

"Believe me that I am in the Father and the Father is in me, or else believe on account of the works themselves. 'Truly, truly, I say to you, whoever believes in me will also do the works that I do, and greater works than these will He do because I am going to the Father. Whatever you ask in my name, this I will do, that the Father may be glorified in the Son.'"

Luke 10:19 ESV

"Behold, I have given you authority to tread on serpents and scorpions, and over all the power of the enemy, and nothing shall hurt you."

Mark 16:17 ESV

"And these signs will accompany those who believe: in my name, they will cast out demons; they will speak in new tongues."

Matthew 17:14-20 ESV

"And when they came to the crowd, a man came up to Him and, kneeling before Him, said, 'Lord, have mercy on my son, for he has seizures and he suffers terribly. For often he falls into the fire, and often into the water. And I brought him to your disciples, and they could not heal him.' And Jesus answered, 'O faithless and twisted generation, how long am I to be with you? How long am I to bear with you? Bring him here to me.' And Jesus rebuked the demon, and it came out of him, and the boy was healed instantly. Then the disciples came to Jesus privately and said, "Why could we not cast it out?' He said to them, 'Because of your little faith. For truly, I say to you, if you have faith like a grain of mustard seed, you will say to this mountain, 'Move from here to there,' and it will move, and nothing will be impossible for you.'"

Romans 8:5-8 ESV

"For those who live according to the flesh set their minds on the things of the flesh, but those who live according to the Spirit set their minds on the things of the spirit. For to set the mind on the flesh is death, but to set the mind on the Spirit is life and peace. For the mind that is set on the flesh is hostile to God, for it does not submit to god's law; indeed, it cannot. Those who are in the flesh cannot please God."

John 10:10 ESV

"The thief comes only to steal and kill and destroy. I came that they may have life and have it abundantly."

Luke 8:2 ESV

"And also, some women who had been healed of evil spirits and infirmities: Mary, called Magdalene, from whom seven demons had gone out."

Matthew 10:1 ESV

"And He called to Him His twelve disciples and gave them authority over unclean spirits, to cast them out, and to heal every disease and every affliction."

Ephesians 6:12 ESV

"For we do not wrestle against flesh and blood, but against the rulers, against the authorities, against the cosmic powers over this present darkness, against the spiritual forces of evil in the heavenly places."

Matthew 8:16 ESV

"That evening they brought to Him many who were oppressed by demons, and He cast out the spirits with a word and healed all who were sick."

John 14:12 ESV

"Truly, truly, I say to you, whoever believes in me will also do the works that I do; and greater works than these will he do because I am going to the father."

Hebrews 2:14 ESV

"Since therefore the children share in flesh and blood, he himself likewise partook of the same things, that through death he might destroy the one who has the power of death, that is, the devil."

Mark 1:27 ESV

"And they were all amazed, so that they questioned among themselves, saying, 'What is this? A new teaching with authority! He commands even the unclean spirits, and they obey Him.'"

Matthew 4:24 ESV

"So, His fame spread throughout all Syria, and they brought Him all the sick, those afflicted with various diseases and pains, those oppressed by demons, epileptics, and paralytics, and He healed them."

Mark 1:34 ESV

"And He healed many who were sick with various diseases and cast out many demons. And He would not permit the demons to speak, because they knew Him."

Mark 9:25 ESV

"And when Jesus saw that a crowd came running together, He rebuked the unclean spirit, saying to it, 'You mute and deaf spirit, I command you, come out of him and never enter him again.'"

John 3:8 ESV

"Whoever makes a practice of sinning is of the devil, for the devil has been sinning from the beginning. The reason the Son of God appeared was to destroy the works of the devil."

Jude 1:9 ESV

"But when the archangel Michael, contending with the devil, was disputing about the body of Moses, he did not presume to pronounce a blasphemous judgment, but said, 'the Lord rebuke you.'"

Luke 4:41 ESV

"And demons also came out of many, crying, 'You are the Son of God!' But He rebuked them and would not allow them to speak, because they knew that He was the Christ."

Luke 11:14 ESV

"Now He was casting out a demon that was mute. When the demon had gone out, the mute man spoke, and the people marveled."

Luke 4:35 ESV

"But Jesus rebuked him, saying, 'Be silent and come out of him!' And when the demon had thrown him down in their midst, he came out of him, having done him no harm."

Luke 8:29 ESV

"For He had commanded the unclean spirit to come out of the man."

Luke 9:1 ESV

"And He called the twelve together and gave them power and authority over all demons and to cure diseases."

Matthew 10:8 ESV

"Heal the sick, raise the dead, cleanse lepers, cast out demons. You received without paying; give without pay."

Mark 6:7 ESV

"And He called the twelve and began to send them out two by two, and gave them authority over the unclean spirits."

Matthew 8:1-34 ESV

"When He came down from the mountain, great crowds followed Him. And behold, a leper came to Him and knelt before Him, saying, 'Lord, if you will, you can make me clean.' And Jesus stretched out His hand and touched him, saying, 'I will; be clean.' And immediately his leprosy was cleansed."

Mark 3:15 ESV

"And have authority to cast out demons."

God is a judicial God with a legal system of laws, with judgments for those who violate His laws. Since it was a man, Adam, who gave away his authority to Satan by his disobedience, it would be a man to legally take it back, paying the penalty for sin while being obedient to the law. God did this through His beloved Son, Jesus, a God-man known as the second Adam. God has given Jesus His final authority in heaven and earth. Jesus said, "All authority in heaven and on earth has been given to me. Therefore, go and make disciples of all nations, baptizing them in the name of the Father and of the Son and of the Holy Spirit" (Matthew 28:18-19 NIV).

It is Jesus who retains ownership of this authority, and He gives this authority to all those who give their life to Him and accept Him as their savior. As believers in Jesus Christ, who covers all our sins by His shed blood on the Cross of Calvary, is the One who makes us whole!

Every believer has the authority, and should always use this authority, to stop Satan in his tracks! "Jesus said, 'I saw Satan fall like lightning from heaven. I have given you authority to trample on snakes and scorpions and to overcome all the power of the enemy; nothing will harm you. However, do not rejoice that the spirits submit to you, but rejoice that your names are written in heaven" (Luke 10:18-20 NIV).

Jesus gives every believer authority to cast out evil spirits, sicknesses, diseases, and even death. For every believer in Christ, death is the beginning of eternal life in God's kingdom. For every non-believer who does not accept Jesus as atonement for their sins, their death only offers eternal pain and suffering in the lake of fire. When we pray, "In the name of Jesus," Satan and his demons will flee every time!

We must know that we, ourselves, can not bind Satan; it is only through the authority of Jesus Christ who can and does. Michael The Archangel, one of God's highest angels, did not personally dare to bind Satan. "But even the Archangel Michael, when he was disputing with the devil about the body of Moses, did not himself dare to condemn him for slander but said, '**the Lord rebuke you**!'" (Jude 1:9 NIV)

By the grace of God, He has given us the authority to bind Satan's power in our lives and others in the name of Jesus. This is through the blood-bought sacrifice of God's Son, Jesus Christ, who paid for all our sins on the Cross of Calvary. Jesus is every believer's powerful authority over Satan and his demons!

Chapter Summary

When Lucifer was created, he was the anointed cherub, the highest angelic creature the Lord ever created. The Lord said to him, "You were the seal of perfection, full of wisdom, and perfect in beauty" (Ezekiel 28:12 NIV). He was perfect in wisdom, with beauty beyond words, a musician, and given the exalted position of hovering over the very throne of God. Upon witnessing all the angelic beings worshiping and praising God and witnessing firsthand the glory and majesty God possessed, Lucifer became insanely jealous of God and no longer wanted to be His servant.

Instead, he coveted all the praise and worship the angelic beings gave to God and wanted this worship for himself. He was obsessed with wanting to be like God, and conceited with the attributes God gave to him. Instead of being grateful for God giving him a highly exalted position, he hated God because he coveted his majesty and the angels worshiping Him day and night. He beguiled himself with the idea of taking over God's throne, majesty, and His entire kingdom. This obsession for supremacy festered so strongly in Satan; it caused him to war against the Almighty God.

Satan can not control himself, and he tempts others to act upon their evil obsessions and impulses. We must be mindful of this and know we should only comply with God's laws and not be tempted with our emotions and desires if they are contrary to keeping God's laws.

Lucifer knew he alone could not battle against our almighty and all-powerful God, but he felt that with help, he could accomplish this impossible feat. Because iniquity abounded so strongly in him, it completely clouded his senses. He devised a plan to seek the help of God's angels to follow him and rebel against God. He convinced one-third of God's angels to follow him in his rebellion to take over God's throne and control His entire kingdom. He was not able to convince the other two-thirds of angelic beings because they chose to honor and worship God and comply with His rulings. Today each of us has this same option to either follow God's laws or follow Satan. The Bible clearly outlines the blessings in following God's laws and the curses in following the evil wiles of Satan. He wants everyone to think we can be like God and independent of Him and His laws and go our separate ways in this life. In actuality, no one can live without God. His very breath in our being is what keeps us alive!

How many angels make up the third of the angels who followed Lucifer? The Bible doesn't give an exact count, but it tells us, "...and the number of them was ten thousand times ten thousand, and thousands of thousands" (Revelation 5:11). Lucifer's obsession to battle for God's supremacy took over any form of rationality or sanity. He was so enamored with pride over his beauty that vanity clouded his judgment.

Unlike Satan, Archangel Michael and his angels were loyal to God and used their power to successfully throw Lucifer and one-third of the angels out of heaven, and down to earth. Satan's ego was damaged tremendously and caused him to have great wrath against God, His angels, and mankind. Satan's obsession is to destroy everyone's life and have them turn against God. This book is meant to counsel everyone to love and obey God, keep His commandments, repent of their sins, and accept Jesus as their Lord and Savior. Then, those who do will have the Blessed Assurance of knowing that you will be counted among those to dwell in God's Kingdom forever. If you follow Satan, you will be numbered with him, his fallen angels, and all those who reject God's amazing grace through His Son, Jesus Christ, will be cast into the eternal fires of hell. The Bible says in hell, the fires are not quenched, and the worms that eat you will not die. "The worms that eat them do not die, and the fire is not quenched" (Mark 9:48 NIV).

CHAPTER FIFTEEN

God's Final Warning to This Generation

The Old Testament Prophet, Isaiah, was given a prophetic warning from God 2700 years ago foretelling him of eerie events that would occur to the last generation before the final events occur in the last days. Scripture confirms the world will soon come to the door of annihilation. But, before this happens, God will send His Son Jesus Christ to rapture every believer who accepted Him as their Savior and atonement for their sins. He will recuse them out of the most cataclysmic events the earth has ever seen before or will ever see again. Today, everyone is witnessing life-changing events that are far from normal globally. The trials and tribulations are piling up with no relief in sight. In trying to adjust to all the upheavals, our governments are making laws and mandates that conflict with our civil and constitutional rights. They are finding it almost impossible to cope with the major issues facing our nation and the world, all at once. Still to come will be even more anarchy worldwide, making rapidly newly arising issues more difficult to resolve.

The reason for all these events happening in succession is a sign that we are drawing nearer to the end of Satan's rulership of planet earth and the Second Coming of Christ. All believers in Jesus Christ will soon be raptured before the final war between God and Satan. After this great battle, all Believers will enter the thousand-year millennium. Non-believers will be thrust into the eternal fires of hell. Jesus commissioned His Apostles to lead souls into God's Kingdom and prepare everyone for the inevitable trials and tribulations that are now pouring out on the entire world. These are the final birth pangs. Jesus told His disciples would occur just before His Second Coming

God spoke to Isaiah of His coming judgment and hope for the last generation:

Isaiah 66 (KJV)

1. Thus saith the Lord, The heaven is my throne, and the earth is my footstool: where is the house that ye build unto me? and where is the place of my rest?

2. For all those things hath mine hand made, and all those things have been, saith the Lord: but to this man will I look, even to him that is poor and of a contrite spirit, and trembleth at my word.

3. He that killeth an ox is as if he slew a man; he that sacrificeth a lamb, as if he cut off a dog's neck; he that offereth an oblation as if he offered swine's blood; he that burneth incense as if he blessed an idol. Yea, they have chosen their own ways, and their soul delighteth in their abominations.

4. I also will choose their delusions, and will bring their fears upon them; because when I called, none did answer; when I spake, they did not hear: but they did evil before mine eyes, and chose that in which I delighted not.

5. Hear the word of the Lord, ye that tremble at His word; Your brethren that hated you, that cast you out for my name's sake, said, Let the Lord be glorified: but He shall appear to your joy, and they shall be ashamed.

6. A voice of noise from the city, a voice from the temple, a voice of the Lord that rendereth recompense to His enemies.

7. Before she travailed, she brought forth; before her pain came, she was delivered of a man child.

8. Who hath heard such a thing? who hath seen such things? Shall the earth be made to bring forth in one day? or shall a nation be born at once? for as soon as Zion travailed, she brought forth her children.

9. Shall I bring to the birth, and not cause to bring forth? saith the Lord: shall I cause to bring forth, and shut the womb? saith thy God.

10. Rejoice ye with Jerusalem, and be glad with her, all ye that love her: rejoice for joy with her, all ye that mourn for her:

11. That ye may suck, and be satisfied with the breasts of her consolations; that ye may milk out, and be delighted with the abundance of her glory.

12. For thus saith the Lord, Behold, I will extend peace to her like a river, and the glory of the Gentiles like a flowing stream: then shall ye suck, ye shall be borne upon her sides, and be dandled upon her knees.

13. As one whom his mother comforteth, so will I comfort you; and ye shall be comforted in Jerusalem.

14. And when ye see this, your heart shall rejoice, and your bones shall flourish like an herb: and the hand of the Lord shall be known toward His servants and indignation toward His enemies.

15. For, behold, the Lord will come with fire, and with His chariots like a whirlwind, to render his anger with fury, and his rebuke with flames of fire.

[16] For by fire and by his sword will the Lord plead with all flesh: and the slain of the Lord shall be many.

[17] They that sanctify themselves, and purify themselves in the gardens behind one tree in the midst, eating swine's flesh, and the abomination, and the mouse, shall be consumed together, saith the Lord.

[18] For I know their works and their thoughts: it shall come, that I will gather all nations and tongues; and they shall come, and see my glory.

[19] And I will set a sign among them, and I will send those that escape of them unto the nations, to Tarshish, Pul, and Lud, that draw the bow, to Tubal, and Javan, to the isles afar off, that have not heard my fame, neither have seen my glory; and they shall declare my glory among the Gentiles.

[20] And they shall bring all your brethren for an offering unto the Lord out of all nations upon horses, and in chariots, and in litters, and upon mules, and upon swift beasts, to my holy mountain Jerusalem, saith the Lord, as the children of Israel bring an offering in a clean vessel into the house of the Lord.

21. And I will also take of them for priests and for Levites, saith the Lord.

22. For as the new heavens and the new earth, which I will make, shall remain before me, saith the Lord, so shall your seed and your name remain.

23. And it shall come to pass, that from one new moon to another, and from one sabbath to another, shall all flesh come to worship before me, saith the Lord.

24. And they shall go forth, and look upon the carcasses of the men that have transgressed against me: for their worm shall not die, neither shall their fire be quenched; and they shall be an abhorring unto all flesh.

The book of Isaiah closes with the sobering and revealing importance of making the right choice about where one will spend eternity, either in Heaven or Hell? Being a believer is the right choice.

CHAPTER SIXTEEN

U.S. Declaration of Independence, Constitution, & Bill of Rights

The Declaration of Independence, The Constitution, and The Bill of Rights are three of the most important documents in American history. President Thomas Jefferson was the principal drafter of The Declaration of Independence. James Madison was the principal drafter of The Constitution and The Bill of Rights. The fundamental rights in our Constitution and the Bill of Rights were created to protect the people's unalienable rights, which our Founding Fathers based on God's Laws, His Ten Commandments, and the Bible. The Declaration of Independence was never amended. The main objective of the thirteen colonies was to break away from England's government over their unfair taxation without representation, exploitation, injustice, tyranny, prohibition of forming any law and being forced to follow rules that were unjust, cruel, and harsh.

The Constitution has been amended twenty-seven times. The First Ten Amendments to The Constitution were the peoples' Bill of Rights, designed to limit the government's harsh rulership over the people. This document was certified on December 15, 1791. These two documents ensure every American their independence and are fundamentally free of being controlled without representation or the natural God-given unalienable rights of life, liberty, and the pursuit of happiness. God created all men to be equal. Our government should guarantee every American their civil and constitutional rights, regardless of race, color, or creed, as stated by President Lincoln, in his Gettysburg Address. The Fourteenth Amendment to the Constitution was ratified in 1868. It declared that not only the Federal Government but every state in the union must constitutionally be required to honor the rights of every American citizen.

Could our Declaration of Independence from England have been foretold prophetically in the book of Daniel as being one of the last days' prophetic messages for our country? This is Daniel's prophetic vision: "The first was like a lion, and it had the wings of an eagle. I watched until its wings were torn off and it was lifted from the ground so that it stood on two feet like a human being, and the mind of a human was given to it" (Daniel 7:4 NIV). England is represented as the lion. The U.S. is represented as the bald eagle. This scripture shows the wings of an eagle torn off the lion and lifted from the ground so that it stood on two feet like a human being and had the mind of a human being. Our Declaration of Independence symbolized our being torn from the lion (England) to stand on our two feet. Doesn't this loudly represent our awesome country? Among all the countries in the world, the United States of America became a great nation because it was founded on the principle of "In God We Trust!" There is no question that God has and still does bless America!

Thomas Jefferson had seventeen days to produce The Declaration of Independence, and yet, he did it in one to two days. This amazing feat was unquestionably divinely inspired.

"We hold these truths to be self-evident, that all men are created equal, that they are endowed by their Creator with certain unalienable Rights, that among these are Life, Liberty and the pursuit of Happiness — That to secure these rights, Governments are instituted among Men, deriving their just powers from the consent of the governed — That whenever any Form of Government becomes destructive of these ends, it is the Right of the People to alter or to abolish it, and to institute new Government, laying its foundation on such principles and organizing its powers in such form, as to them shall seem most likely to effect their Safety and Happiness."

The idea that all men are created equal came to take on a life of its own and is today considered a perfect foundation of the American creed.

In 1863, Abraham Lincoln declared, "Four score and seven years ago our fathers brought forth on this continent, a new nation, conceived in Liberty, and dedicated to the proposition that all men are created equal."

Years earlier, on the anniversary of George Washington's birthday in 1861, President Lincoln said, "...I would rather be assassinated on this spot [Independence Hall] than to surrender it [the principles of the Declaration of Independence]." The Declaration of Independence was a document stating why the colonists were breaking away from England. It did not give any rights to anyone. Even though it wasn't a legal document, the Founding Fathers signed it anyway, stating, "For the support of this Declaration, with a firm reliance on the protection of divine Providence, we mutually pledge to each other our Lives, our Fortunes, and our sacred Honor."

It took the Civil War, the bloodiest war in American history, for Lincoln to make Thomas Jefferson's vision of equality a Constitutional reality. Thirteenth, Fourteenth, and Fifteenth Amendments to The Constitution are known as "The Reconstruction Amendments." They extended new Constitutional protections to African Americans.

The Thirteenth Amendment was passed by Congress on January 31, 1865, and ratified on December 6, 1865.

> "Neither slavery nor involuntary servitude, except as a punishment for crime whereof the party shall have been duly convicted, shall exist within the United States, or any place subject to their jurisdiction. Congress shall have the power to enforce this article by appropriate legislation."

The Fourteenth Amendment was passed by Congress on June 13, 1866, and ratified on July 9, 1868.

> "All persons born or naturalized in the United States, and subject to the jurisdiction thereof, are citizens of the United States and of the State wherein they reside. No State shall make or enforce any law which shall abridge the privileges or immunities of citizens of the United States; nor shall any State deprive any person of life, liberty, or property, without due process of law; nor deny to any person within its jurisdiction the equal protection of the laws. Representatives shall be apportioned among the several States according to their respective numbers, counting the whole number of persons in each State, excluding Indians not taxed.

But when the right to vote at any election for the choice of electors for President and Vice-President of the United States, Representatives in Congress, the Executive and Judicial officers of a State, or the members of the Legislature thereof, is denied to any of the male inhabitants of such State, being twenty-one years of age, and citizens of the United States, or in any way abridged, except for participation in rebellion, or other crime, the basis of representation therein shall be reduced in the proportion which the number of such male citizens shall bear to the whole number of male citizens twenty-one years of age in such State. No person shall be a Senator or Representative in Congress, or elector of President and Vice-President, or hold any office, civil or military, under the United States, or under any State, who, having previously taken an oath, as a member of Congress, or as an officer of the United States, or as a member of any State legislature, or as an executive or judicial officer of any State, to support the Constitution of the United States, shall have engaged in insurrection or rebellion against the same, or given aid or comfort to the enemies thereof. But Congress may, by a vote of two-thirds of each House, remove such disability. The validity of the public debt of the United States, authorized by law, including debts incurred for payment of pensions and bounties for services in suppressing insurrection or rebellion, shall not be questioned. But neither the United States nor any State shall assume or pay any debt or obligation incurred in aid of insurrection or rebellion against the United States, or any claim for the loss or emancipation of any slave; but all such debts, obligations, and claims shall be held illegal and void. The Congress shall have the power to enforce, by appropriate legislation, the provisions of this article."

The Fifteenth Amendment was passed by Congress on February 26, 1869, and ratified on February 3, 1870.

"The right of citizens of the United States to vote shall not be denied or abridged by the United States or by any State on account of race, color, or previous condition of servitude. The Congress shall have the power to enforce this article by appropriate legislation."

These Amendments to The Constitution all conveyed that people have certain unalienable and inherent rights that come from God, not the government. When people give the government those rights over them, it takes away our natural and unalienable rights of enjoyment of life, liberty, the pursuit of happiness, and safety. This includes the right to possess and protect property, the right to a majority of the people, and the right to alter and abolish their government whenever it threatens to invade their natural rights rather than protect them.

Advocating The Bill of Rights, Thomas Jefferson wrote to James Madison, March 15, 1789, "Half a loaf is better than no bread. If we cannot secure all our rights, let us secure what we can."

**The United States Bill of Rights:
The First Ten Amendments to The Constitution**

First Amendment

Congress shall make no law respecting an establishment of religion, or prohibiting the free exercise thereof; or abridging the freedom of speech, or of the press, or the right of the people peaceably to assemble, and to petition the government for a redress of grievances.

Second Amendment

A well-regulated militia, being necessary to the security of a free state, the right of the people to keep and bear arms, shall not be infringed.

Third Amendment

No soldier shall, in time of peace, be quartered in any house, without the consent of the owner; nor in time of war, but in a manner to be prescribed by law.

Fourth Amendment

The right of the people to be secure in their persons, houses, papers, and effects, against unreasonable searches and seizures, shall not be violated, and no Warrants shall issue, but upon probable cause, supported by oath or affirmation, and particularly describing the place to be searched, and the persons or things to be seized.

Fifth Amendment

No person shall be held to answer for a capital, or

otherwise, infamous crime, unless on a presentment or indictment of a grand jury, except in cases arising in the land or naval forces, or in the militia, when in actual service in time of war or public danger; nor shall any person be subject for the same offense to be twice put in jeopardy of life or limb; nor shall be compelled in any criminal case to be a witness against himself; nor be deprived of life, liberty, or property, without due process of law; nor shall private property be taken for public use without just compensation.

Sixth Amendment
In all criminal prosecutions, the accused shall enjoy the right to a speedy and public trial, by an impartial jury of the state and district wherein the crime shall have been committed; which district shall have been previously ascertained by law, and be informed of the nature and cause of the accusation; to be confronted with the witnesses against him; to have compulsory process for obtaining witnesses in his favor; and to have the assistance of counsel for his defense.

Seventh Amendment
In suits at common law, where the value in controversy shall exceed twenty dollars, the right of trial by jury shall be preserved, and no fact tried by a jury shall be otherwise reexamined in any court of the united states, then according to the rules of common law.

Eighth Amendment

Excessive bail shall not be required, nor excessive fines imposed, nor cruel and unusual punishments inflicted.

Ninth Amendment

The enumeration in the constitution of certain rights shall not be construed to deny or disparage others retained by the people.

Tenth Amendment

The powers not delegated to the united states by the constitution, nor prohibited by it to the states, are reserved to the States respectively, or to the people.

The Declaration of Independence, The Constitution, and The Bill of Rights represent the ideas that define the American people as a nation under God.

The Preamble [introductory statement] of The U.S. Constitution

"We the People of the United States, in order to form a more perfect Union, establish Justice, insure domestic Tranquility, provide for the common defense, promote the general Welfare, and secure the Blessings of Liberty to ourselves and our Posterity, do ordain and establish this Constitution for the United States of America."

The opening of The Declaration of Independence

"We hold these truths to be self-evident, that all men are created equal, that they are endowed by their Creator with certain unalienable Rights, that among these are Life, Liberty and the pursuit of Happiness."

Thomas Jefferson knew the Right of Revolution had to be exercised when a government threatened the natural rights of the people, given to every human being by God.

Our God-given rights are life, liberty, and property. Our Biblical human rights include freedom, equality, and dignity. God's rights are not earned but divinely ordained because we are made in His likeness and image.

"Teacher, which is the greatest commandment in the Law? Jesus replied: 'Love the Lord your God with all your heart and with all your soul and with all your mind.' This is the first and greatest commandment. And the second is like it: 'Love your neighbor as yourself.' All the Law and the Prophets hang on these two commandments" (Matthew 22:36-40 NIV).

Exactly what Jesus told His apostles two thousand years ago still stands today. God's Ten Commandments can not be amended or changed by man. God's Laws command everyone to love Him and each other. When we abide by these two Commandments, this covers the whole law for mankind! Our Founding Fathers based the Declaration of Independence, The Constitution, and The Bill of Rights on God's Ten Commandments and the Bible. We the people and citizens of this great country must always keep God first in our lives and our country. Then, God will pour His blessings on us all!

CHAPTER SEVENTEEN

Three Lake County Sheriff Deputies Brutally Beat My Son

On October 5, 2015, minutes after 11:00 am, I was having my daily Bible study while listening to my audio cd on the Old and New Testament. I was in my master suite when I heard a deafening scream for help and cries of pain coming from the living area. I rushed into the living room and was in total shock seeing three Lake County Sheriff Deputies beating, kicking, and punching my son over his entire body. He was lying face down on the floor, just inside the foyer entrance. He was screaming in pain while three-armed men were brutally assaulting him. My first thought was disbelief that this could be happening, and this must be a nightmare! My second thought was to call the police. But police officers were the ones assaulting my son. I yelled repeatedly for the officers to stop beating my son!!! They ignored my pleas and continued brutally assaulting him like crazed animals on a kill. Terror and fear overwhelmed me! At almost 79 years of age, I had never personally witnessed such violence before in my entire life!

The Lord gave me the instant wisdom and strength to run back into my bedroom, grab my cell phone, and record the deputies' physical abuse on my fifty-four-year-old son, Robert

Anthony, on the cell phone video. He was the only surviving member of our family. My husband and two daughters had passed away two years earlier, all within one year and fifty-five days. Robert and I were the only surviving members of our close-knit Christian family. The deputies' beating was so severe, that I thought they were going to kill my son before my very own eyes. The fear from this brutal assault on my son covered all my senses. They were brutally attacking him repeatedly all over his head, face, and body. Two of the three officers were on each side of him, while the third officer was bodily holding down his legs, watching as the other two deputies repeatedly assaulted my son. Robert was screaming out with excruciating pain as the deputies were brutally inflicting repeated blows to his body as he lay defenseless on the floor. Their beating was so severe, that it drew blood from Robert's face, head, and upper torso. They ripped his t-shirt down below his chest, exposing the punch marks on his neck, ears, chest, and back. One officer was repeatedly field kicking him on the left side of his body to his ribs and abdomen. The second officer, kneeling on the right side of my son, was repeatedly punching him in his face, head, ears, and eyes. The third officer laid bodily on Robert's legs, suppressing and holding him down, while watching the other two deputies brutally assault my son, non-stop! Words alone can not describe the depth of my heartache, witnessing this brutal beating on my son.

They kept Robert handcuffed for close to ten hours, keeping him upright on a straight chair while he was in severe pain, battered, bruised, bleeding, and in traumatic shock. They did this without having a search warrant. After the assault, and after they searched our entire home, is when an officer went to get a search warrant. I was physically restrained from leaving the area near the front door or using my landline phone to call an attorney.

I didn't want to use my cell phone for fear they would take it and erase the video showing evidence of their brutal beating. The deputies demanded Robert and I stay by the front entry door to our living room while they freely roamed around the house doing a warrantless search without any probable cause.

I had never used the video camera on my cell phone in this manner before. It was an absolute miracle that I recorded over thirty-five minutes of the aftermath of the deputies' brutal assault. The video successfully captured evidence of their illegal search without a search warrant, and Captain XXXX's unlawful command to Robert, demanding the key to his locked bedroom closet door. His unlawful command of doing an unlawful search without a warrant was recorded on my cell phone video. The deputy who blinded my son on his left eye was also recorded on the video saying, "This beating happened to your son because he wouldn't let us come in and search the property." I answered, "Without a search warrant, I don't blame him. No one would let you in!"

Several hours later, at 6:30 pm, a deputy arrived with a signed search warrant by a Magistrate Judge. The three deputies' severe assault on my son escalated my blood pressure to a dangerous level causing me to become light-headed and nauseous. Knowing the state of anguish my son and I were in, the deputies called in the EMTs. When they arrived, Deputy XXXX, who repeatedly kicked my son on the left side of his ribs and stomach, met the EMTs at the front door asking for a band-aid to cover his bleeding fist. (this was recorded on the cell phone video)

One of the EMTs examined me and said my blood pressure was 222 over 102 and that I could go into a stroke at any time and should be transported immediately to the hospital. (this was recorded on my cell phone video.) I refused to go to the hospital and leave my son alone with these deputies, fearing for his life. Their beating was so severe, I thought they were going to kill him!!! When the EMTs wanted my son to go to the hospital, he feared leaving me alone and said he was okay, so they wouldn't force him to go to the hospital. Moments later, I asked Robert, fearing for the beaten state he was in, "Robert, are you all right?" He said, "No, I'm not all right." (This was recorded on the cell phone video.) Viewing my son's face, head, and body, which showed the bloody evidence of their brutal assault, made me very ill.

While waiting several hours for the warrant, the officers took complete control of our home. They were walking freely into every room, opening closets, doors, and drawers, laughing, drinking their beverages, and joking with each other as my son and I were held captive. Being in severe pain, my son was forced to sit upright in a straight chair, tightly handcuffed behind his back, for close to ten hours. After searching the home, the deputies were frustrated they could not find any evidence of a hand-held computer. I knew their warrantless search had not only violated our Fourth Amendment rights, but their brutal beating was in violation of Federal Civil Rights Law Section 1983 (42 USC 1983). Breaking the law didn't seem to bother them at all. They all appeared confident and superior. The one who beat and kicked my son was smug and arrogant. I took a picture of him on my cell phone after he had just brutally beaten and kicked my son.

After searching our entire home and not finding the hand-held computer, the only door they couldn't open was my son's locked bedroom closet. Captain XXXX, being visibly upset about not finding the hand-held computer, which is what they were looking for, made an unlawful command and angrily threatened my son. He said, "Robert if you don't give me the key to the locked door in your bedroom, I'll have the deputies kick the door off its hinges." (I recorded his threat on my cell phone video.)

Out of sheer fear, my son, still tightly handcuffed behind his back, sitting now on the floor, badly bruised, bloodied, and hurting from pain over his entire body, told Captain XXXX where the key was. They opened the closet door and found all my deceased husband's electronic equipment, including his sawed-off rifle and the hand-held computer. The deputy's body-worn camcorder recorded him saying, "We found it! There it is!" This camcorder was evidence against them for doing an unlawful search and seizure without a search warrant because it recorded the date and time of their unlawful search as being 11:37 am on October 5, 2015. The warrant wasn't signed by a magistrate until after 5:00 pm that same day.

All they wanted was to justify their illegal entry, brutal beating, and searching of our home without a warrant. They did this by staging the handheld computer they found in a locked bedroom closet. Then their police report falsely stated they found the hand-held computer in plain view to justify their search without a warrant. After the deputies found the handheld computer, they unzipped the case, placed it on the bed, and plugged the hand-held computer into a wall socket. They called in CSI to take pictures of their staged crime scene and then falsely stated on their police report that the hand-held computer was in plain view. All this evidence of their unlawful search was recorded on their body-worn camcorders.

I knew I had to preserve the cell phone video, hire a criminal attorney for my son, and get my cell phone out of the house before they took it from me and erased the evidence of all their criminal violations. Fear alone prompted me to preserve the only evidence I had against their unlawful entry, the brutal beating of my son, and the warrantless search of our home. My blood pressure was escalating and started to overwhelm me. I told the deputies I was very ill and wanted to drive myself to the hospital, as the EMT had earlier recommended. This was the only way they would let me leave the house with my cell phone still in my hand.

As I was leaving, I looked over at Robert, who was in such pain, sitting on the straight chair, tightly handcuffed behind his back, dazed and bleeding from their brutal beating. Seeing his anguish tore open my heart. All I could think of was to help and heal my son and get my cell phone video out of the house. I needed to hire a criminal attorney and then go to the hospital. Going into shock or dying was not an option for me.

While driving to the hospital, my blood pressure was so high I needed to spiritually fortify myself to keep going forward. I pulled over to the side of the road, called three criminal lawyers in Mt. Dora, FL, and left messages for them to call me back. One lawyer called within minutes. Upon telling him what happened, he stated, "They are doing this ass-backward. Let them take whatever they want, and I'll have it thrown out." After he told me the deputies broke the law, I asked if he could sue them. He said, "I know these guys personally; if I sue them, they will plant drugs in my car. But I can get you someone who can sue them for you. You are lucky they didn't take your cell phone and erase the video."

ROBERT'S HELL ON EARTH

The Torment Begins

Our beautiful home in Mt. Dora, FL. For more than ten years, it represented a family refuge for peace and tranquility. That peace was forever **SHATTERED** on the morning of October 5, 2015 as three Lake County Sheriff's Deputies illegally forced their way through the front door, without a Warrant or any Exigent Circumstances, and proceeded to savagely beat Robert, causing his physical disability.

Just inside the front door of our Mt. Dora, FL home as it was moments before the Lake County Sherriff's Deputies pushed through the door after **Robert legally declined their request to search the house WITHOUT A SEARCH WARRANT!** This photo also clearly shows that with the shutters closed, as they were on October 5, 2015, no one, including the police, could see through the doors or windows to claim they had "Exigent Circumstances" to forcefully enter the home.

It was on this very floor, just a few feet from the door, that Robert was beaten, bloodied, and blinded by the three Deputies from the Lake County Sherriff's Department as he laid face down on the floor, in a submissive, prone position.

Robert's Bedroom – On the left side of the picture you can see the closet door that was locked when the Deputies unlawfully entered the house. They threatened to kick the door off its hinges if Robert did not give them the key. This is the room in which they staged the "Crime Scene" to make it appear as if the laptop was **"in plain view."**

On the right side of the photo above you can see a framed picture hanging on the wall. The picture is a beautiful pencil sketch, "The Face of God." That is the only picture or photograph *"in plain view"* **when the Deputies entered Robert's bedroom.**

Above, Deputies swarm around Robert, already in handcuffs, as the punching and kicking stops and he is pulled into a sitting position, **the very moment I started to record their unlawful beating.**

Below, Robert, clearly frightened, tries to understand what is happening inside our home!

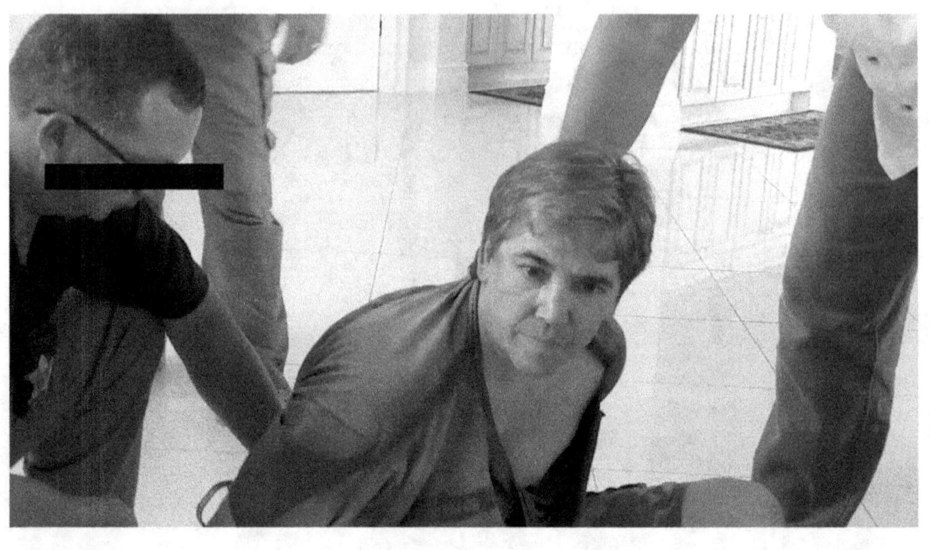

Above, Deputies continue to stand in a tight perimeter around Robert, even though he is sitting cross-legged, and handcuffed on the floor, receiving treatment from the EMTs for injuries caused by the Deputies beating.

Below, with his t-shirt ripped down the front, the cuts and bruises from the brutal assault by law enforcement officers, are very visible.

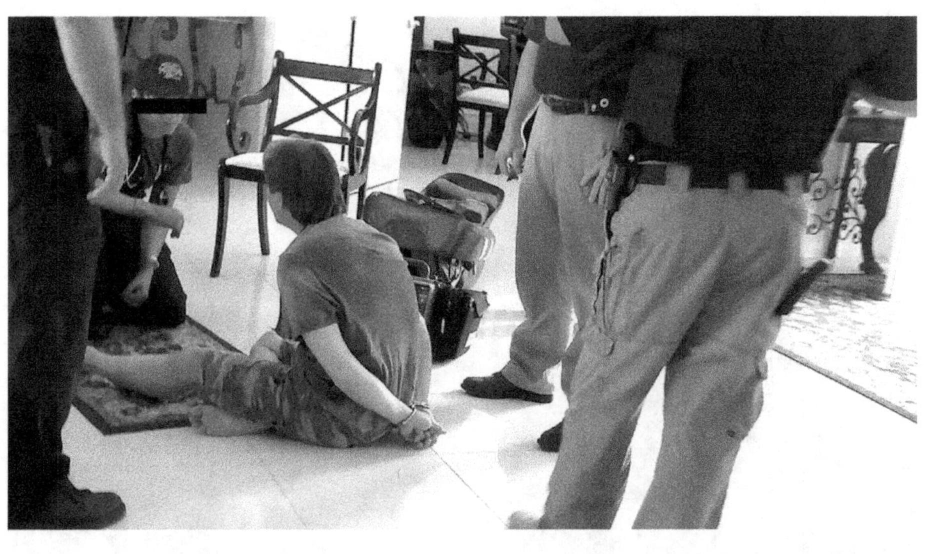

Above and below: The cuts and bruises from the injuries Robert sustained during the vicious bashing from the Sherriff's Deputies to his head and face are clearly visible.

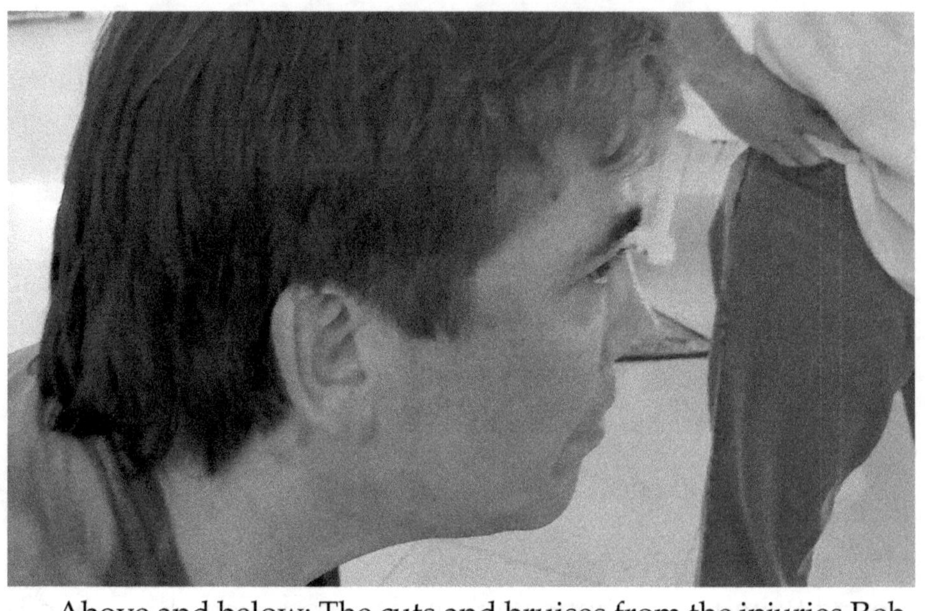

Right, Robert's Official Booking Photo taken the night of October 5, 2015 at the Lake County Detention Center. He was finally transferred there after being forced to endure 10+ hours of agonizing pain from the injuries, extra-tight handcuffs and being denied any food and water.

Robert was finally released on Bond on October 9, 2015. In the weeks that followed, he and I would spend virtually every minute together, both for his safety and mine. This picture to the right was taken shortly after his release. As you can see, the contusions around his eyes have now fully formed, as the tiny blood vessels, called capillaries, burst from the trauma of his beating and the blood pooling just under the skin.

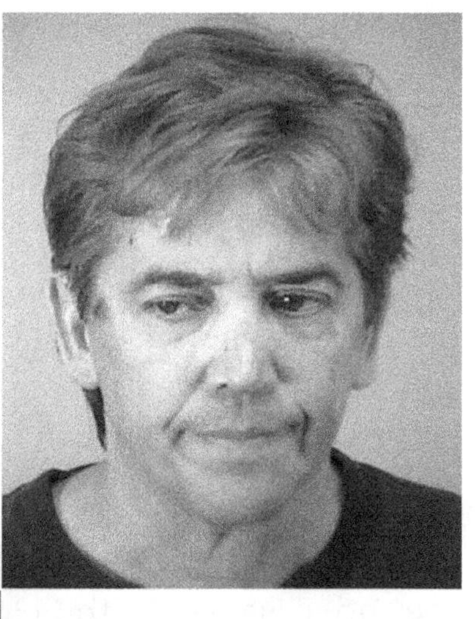

With this attorney confirming my fear of losing the only evidence I had, my cell phone video, I detoured from going to the hospital and drove directly to a Radio Shack to preserve the video and transfer it to an application I had on my computer. During the drive to Radio Shack, the second attorney called and said she was a former state prosecuting attorney for three years. She said the officers had broken the law and also police protocol by their actions and wanted to handle the case against them to defend my son's rights. She said in her career of being a prosecutor, she never lost a case.

I arrived at the Radio Shack and hurried into the store to have the video saved to the cloud. While there, the third attorney called. After I told him what happened and where I was, he said he was nearby and would meet me at the Radio Shack. He confirmed what the other two attorneys said, that the deputies violated my son's Fourth Amendment rights, and their search and seizure was illegal. All three attorneys stated, that whatever the officers took by their unlawful search was fruit from a poisonous tree and cannot be used in a court of law. The attorney came back to the house with me to speak with Robert. When we entered the home, Robert was still handcuffed behind his back, sitting uncomfortably on the straight chair. His face and eyes were now visibly swollen and bruised from the punch marks along with open cuts that had bled down his face and upper torso. The lawyer asked, "Robert, are you alright."

He said, "No, I'm not all right, I'm in a lot of pain, and I can't see out of my left eye." He looked over to me and said, "Mom, while you were away, the deputies called in CSI to take pictures of my bedroom. They're still in there." As they were leaving, I asked the CSI photographer to take pictures of my son's beaten body. I pulled up Robert's t-shirt, which was torn down to underneath his heart, exposing the open bloody wounds and punch marks on his upper torso, front, and back. I had them also take pictures of the bloody open wounds on his head, face, neck, and ears. The deputy who tore his t-shirt, and kicked and punched him repeatedly, stood nearby in hearing distance of Robert talking to his attorney. After witnessing Robert's beating, the attorney said, "I want to handle this case for Robert."

The deputies kept Robert captive from 11:00 am, until 10:30 pm before taking him to the Lake County Detention Center. Another officer arrived and put chains on Robert's waist, wrist and ankles and locked his handcuffs now in front of him. His wrists were all reddened from a lack of circulation after wearing the tightly secured handcuffs for over ten hours behind his back while sitting in a straight chair. My heart was pierced as I watched him walk out the door, chained, physically bruised and battered, and in a great deal of pain. Never in Robert's entire life was he ever in police custody for anything

Robert endured this traumatic encounter with these three Sheriff Deputies with such strength of character. He never once used any force or resistance or showed any disrespect for the officers; he only spoke of how much pain he was in. The Deputies filed a false charge against Robert of resisting an officer without violence. Our Founding Fathers created the U.S. Constitution and the Bill of Rights so that no American citizen should ever have to go through what my son was subjected to by these three Lake County Sheriff's Deputies. No American citizen should ever have to live through such reprehensible abuse by any police officer!

From 11:00 am until 12:00 midnight, the deputies had full control of our home. They relaxed on my two white sofas, talking, laughing, and making jokes with each other. Then, around midnight they finally left. Alone, I was capsized with profound sorrow for what my son had just gone through. I laid down on my bed with my heart pounding and broken. Even in my exhausted state, I couldn't keep my eyes closed. I got up after a few moments and went back into the living room. I sat on the white hassock next to my grand piano and looked at the scene where the deputies brutally assaulted my son.

Just then, I heard a very profound and deep resonating voice in my spirit, "Virginia, that's how I felt when they beat up my Son and crucified Him on the cross." At that moment, the presence of God being with me was so desperately and profoundly needed! His words made me realize, for the first time in my entire life, the depth of His pain and sorrow when He, too, witnessed His own Son being brutally beaten. God showed me at that moment His own broken heart when He sacrificed His Son for the sins of the whole world. For the first time in my devout Christian life, I truly realized what it cost God and Jesus to save humanity from their eternal judgment for sin, in the fires of hell.

John 3:16 is probably the most well-known Bible verse: "For God so loved the world that He gave His one and only Son, that whoever believes in Him shall not perish but have eternal life" (NIV). This is why Jesus, out of love for humanity, gave up His own life willingly to save the entire human race and bring us all home into God's eternal paradise in heaven.

I was now physically alone, and for the first time in my entire life, and had to deal with emotions I never knew existed in my being. They were so profound and overwhelming. I had to feed those devastating feelings with positive ones. I did this with prayer and determination to God to seek freedom for my son and justice through the courts. I was given a power greater than words can explain to go through what my son and I had to endure to seek freedom and justice for the 1011 days he was incarcerated in a Detention Center without a trial or any form of justice. I knew spiritually and, in my mind, I was never alone because I held on to the knowledge that God never leaves or forsakes us. These Scriptures in the King James Bible empowered me through the hardships I had to endure to fight for justice and save my son's life:

Deuteronomy 31:8
"And the Lord, he it is that doth go before thee; he will be with thee, he will not fail thee, neither forsake thee: fear not, neither be dismayed."

Deuteronomy 31:6
"And the Lord, he it is that doth go before thee; he will be with thee, he will not fail thee, neither forsake thee: fear not, neither be dismayed."

Isaiah 41:10-13
"Fear thou not; for I am with thee: be not dismayed; for I am thy God: I will strengthen thee; yea, I will help thee; yea, I will uphold thee with the right hand of my righteousness. Behold, all they that were incensed against thee shall be ashamed and confounded: they shall be as nothing, and they that strive with thee shall perish. Thou shalt seek them, and shalt not find them, even them that contended with thee: they that war against thee shall be as nothing, and as a thing of naught. For I the Lord thy God will hold thy right hand, saying unto thee, Fear not; I will help thee."

1 Peter 5:7

"Casting all your care upon him; for he careth for you."

Hebrews 13:6

"So that we may boldly say, The Lord is my helper, and I will not fear what man shall do unto me."

Psalms 55:22

"Cast thy burden upon the Lord, and He shall sustain thee: He shall never suffer the righteous to be moved."

Romans 8:28

"And we know that all things work together for good to them that love God, to them who are the called according to His purpose."

2 Timothy 1:7

"For God hath not given us the spirit of fear; but of power, and of love, and of a sound mind."

Hebrews 4:16

"Let us, therefore, come boldly unto the throne of grace, that we may obtain mercy, and find grace to help in time of need."

1 Chronicles 28:20

"And David said to Solomon his son, Be strong and of good courage, and do it: fear not, nor be dismayed: for the Lord God, even my God, will be with thee; He will not fail thee, nor forsake thee until thou hast finished all the work for the service of the house of the LORD."

Not once did I allow my mind to think anything but faith in God that my son would be exonerated and have justice for his fifty-four years of living a good life! Whatever it took to seek freedom and justice for my son was now my full-time quest.

In the morning, I called the jail and was told I could not speak to or visit my son because he had to give written permission to the jail for me to visit him. I asked, "How can I get written permission if I can't see or talk to him?"

He said, "You can write him a letter." I immediately sent out an overnight letter, which came back days later undelivered.

During the evening of my second night alone, my doorbell rang at 9:00 pm. I looked through the shutters and saw a tall black man standing outside my front door. I yelled out, "Who are you?"

He said, "I'm a tv reporter from XXXX station and want to interview you about your son."

I said, "No! How did you get into this gated community?"

He said, "I can't say."

I told him to leave and put his card thru the garage door mail slot. He did and left. My heart was still pounding with fear as I checked all the doors and windows in the 6,000 sq. ft. home I had designed and built for my family in 2007. I kept praying to God to get me through this nightmare and bring my son home.

My husband, Daniel Ortung, and I were together for forty-five years before he passed away at the age of seventy-five, on September 30, 2013, from stage 4 cancer. Two years before this incident occurred. He worked as a Florida licensed private investigator. He handled mostly family and domestic cases. He used a wide range of surveillance equipment, including tripods, laptop computers, cameras, video equipment, and weapons he was licensed to carry. When he passed away, my son kept all his electronic equipment and weapons locked in his bedroom closet.

When these electronics were found by the deputies, they used some of my husband's electronics as evidence against my son.

Anne Marie, my eldest daughter, was fifty-four years old when she passed away on September 17, 2012, just a year earlier than my husband. Fifty-five days after Dan's passing, my middle daughter, Patty Lynne, also fifty-four years old, passed away with stage 4 cancer. Their passing was a shock to both me and Robert. Never could I imagine, with all I'd been through, that I would be facing such bogus criminalized behavior perpetrated on my son from these three Lake County Sheriff Deputies.

On the fourth day of my son being in jail, a bail bondsman called and said, "Ms. O'Hare, I'm here with your son. He is worried about you. I can have Robert out on bond immediately for a $13,500 bond fee."

I was elated and said, "Yes, come right over."

When he arrived, I was being interviewed by two news reporters from local tv stations. The bail bondsman said, "I have an attorney you can hire for your son. He is one of the ten best criminal lawyers in the state of Florida."

I told him I was getting ready to hire a former prosecutor who was coming to my home within hours. He said, "No, I'll call him right now, and he will come to you." Due to this bail bondsman helping my son, I consented to meet with the attorney.

After meeting with the lawyer, he confirmed what the other three attorneys had said, that the deputies broke the law by violating my son's Fourth Amendment rights, and "Whatever they get will be *fruit from a poisonous tree*, they can't use it. There was nothing in plain view that the deputies could see to justify their forcing their way into your home and beating up your son." After viewing my cell phone video, he said, "I need a copy of that video by tomorrow morning. That's our ace in the hole."

The lawyer and the bail bondsman were very helpful and speedy in bailing out my son. At 11:00 pm that evening, the attorney brought my son home and said, "I feel even better about this case after meeting your son. He's a wholesome, nice-looking, clean-cut man." I was more than elated to see my son after his horrible ordeal in jail for the first time in his fifty-four years of life. He never had any violations. He didn't drink or smoke, or take drugs. Our family always lived according to our Christian belief standards.

After my son arrived home, he said, "Mom, I prayed to God repeatedly for four hours to let me come home and sleep in my own bed by 11:30 pm." God answered my son's prayers. He was home and in his own bed by 11:30 pm that same night! Robert's lawyer advised Robert and me to leave Mt. Dora immediately and go to our home in Ft. Lauderdale to be safe from the Sheriff Deputies! He, like the other attorneys, knew of the deputies' reputation in the community. So, we left the following day and stayed five months in our Ft. Lauderdale home, an upscale waterfront gated and armed-guard community. I festered over my son being brutally beaten and all the intestinal pain and blindness to his left eye during that time. He was still suffering from health issues from their beating. I couldn't get back to our Mt. Dora home soon enough to file a criminal complaint with the Lake County Internal Affairs against the three Sheriff's Deputies. I met with the Lake County Internal Affairs investigator and his supervisor. They both listened intently and wanted to interview my son as soon as possible.

The next morning, both arrived at our Mt. Dora home and recorded Robert's details of his abuse. He said, "The deputies came to our front door and asked if they could search our home. I asked if they had a search warrant.

The deputy answered, "No, we do not have a search warrant."

I said," Get a search warrant, and I'll call my lawyer. I proceeded to close the door. The three deputies forced open the door, stepped into our home, and physically attacked me. One deputy punched me in the stomach and knocked me to the floor. Then all three deputies ganged up on me. Two of the deputies were on each side of me. The blond hair deputy started kicking and punching me over my body, ribs, and stomach. The other deputy kneeling on my right side kept punching me in my head, face, and eyes while the third deputy, the bald-headed deputy, laid on my legs so the other two could beat me up. The deputy on my left side kept punching and kicking me ten or twelve times to my ribs and stomach. He roughly tore my t-shirt from behind, leaving burn marks on my neck. The deputy on my right side was kneeling and using his fist to repeatedly hit me in my head, face, eyes, and ears. He kept poking me repeatedly with his fist. This caused blindness in my left eye. The pain in the eye was severe and constant. Their beating caused intestinal bleeding and a great deal of pain in my ribs and abdomen. Since my beating five months ago, I'm still bleeding from my bowel movements and have to take laxatives and coffee enemas to move my bowels."

After ongoing suffering from the brutal beating, Robert developed pre-cancerous polyps that spawned into stage 4 colon cancer. During emergency surgery, Robert had a colostomy bag placed on the same side where the deputy kicked him on October 5, 2015.

I told the supervisor that my son also takes coffee enemas regularly to move his bowel. A physician told Robert his ruptured ribs would heal on their own, which they did months later….

Several months before Robert's assault, he had a drum surgically implanted in his left eye to secure a torn retina so he wouldn't go blind. The deputy who repeatedly punched Robert in his eyes dislodged the drum in his left eye and caused unbearable pain due to the drum becoming wrinkled from the assault on his eyes. Robert had two eye surgeries to try and regain his vision. Both of these two surgeries were unsuccessful. The third surgery was scheduled for ninety days later, but this never happened because the deputies gave false testimony to the judge stating my son was a danger to the community, so the judge revoked his bond on August 25, 2016, and added other bogus charges and an arrest warrant against my son was issued.

On August 25, 2016, as we left our Ft. Lauderdale residence, Robert was driving us to lunch when a truck started to tailgate us. Not knowing who this was, we drove down the next street to see if the truck would follow us. It did, then another truck came upon us and hit our vehicle broadside on the passenger side. This truck was driven by a police officer, who later told me this was his first week as a police officer, and he jumped out of his truck with his gun in his hand and forgot to secure his clutch in the park position. He used a crowbar to break the side window of our parked car for no apparent reason. Robert and I sat motionless in the front seat as glass particles splattered all over the inside of the car. If God had not given my son and me the strength and willpower to go through all this, we both would have collapsed from sheer fear. Thank God we both kept our heads as the Holy Spirit gave us wisdom, strength, and perseverance to endure this second police encounter, only ten months later.

Another officer shouted on his megaphone to Robert while we were still sitting in the car, "Put your hands up over your head, and get out of the car and lie face down." Robert did exactly what he was told. He got out of the car and laid face down on the hot pavement. Then the officer, who hit our vehicle with his truck, fell bodily on Robert's left shoulder and demanded, "Put your hands behind your back."

I yelled at the officer, "How can he put his left hand behind his back with your 200 lbs. lying on his shoulder?"

Then the officer yelled to Robert, "Stop resisting!"

I yelled back at the officer, "He is not resisting; he's face down on the pavement." Then another officer pulled Robert up bodily from the ground and dropped him face down on the concrete pavement causing Robert severe abdominal pain, which he still had from his beating 10 months prior, and scratching his face, knees, arms, and body. During this abuse, Robert was still suffering health issues from the first police beating ten months earlier. He had severe pain in his ribs and abdomen and was bleeding from his bowel movements. This rough treatment only exacerbated his already chronic abdominal pain and intestinal problems. Witnessing this again for the second time was heart rendering. I took pictures of the officer's abuse of Robert's face and body and of the tragic police scene. Then, I called Robert's lawyer and handed my cell phone over to the U.S. Marshal in charge. He told Robert's lawyer, "We are charging Robert with resisting an office without violence because we used force." Robert was in unbearable abdominal pain. Seeing the harm they created, the officers drove Robert immediately to Imperial Point Hospital in Ft. Lauderdale, Fl, where my son was diagnosed with pre-cancerous bleeding polyps in his colon and instructed him to see a GI doctor for a colonoscopy within three days. Upon being transported back to the Lake County detention center, the Lake County Judge never honored Robert's motions to the Court for urgent medical treatment for his pre-cancerous bleeding polyps.

The Ordeal Continues

Shortly after the incident at our Mt. Dora FL home, Robert and I returned to our second home in Ft. Lauderdale, FL. (above) On the morning of August 17, 2016, we left home as usual, to run a few errands and have a quiet lunch together. As soon as we were out of the driveway, I noticed a big dark-blue SUV following us very closely. I asked Robert to turn down the next street, but the SUV continued to follow us. Robert stopped the car near the curb. Just then, the SUV SPED UP and smashed into the passenger side of our car! Several seconds later, several other unmarked cars completely encircled us.

A voice from a police megaphone ordered Robert to raise his hands, exit the vehicle and lay flat on the cement road.

After Robert complied, an officer lifted him up and bodily dropped him face down on the hot cement pavement. Just then, another officer fell with his full body weight on Robert's left shoulder yelling, "Stop Resisting! Stop Resisting!" He was not resisting, but in a submissive, prone position, ready to be handcuffed. Such physical brutality caused Robert abdominal pain and intestinal bleeding. After this officer filed a false resisting charge, a Broward County Jury exonerated Robert from those false resisting charges.

This totally unnecessary collision was so severe that it bent the rear axle of my car, rendering it unsafe to drive. I replaced it with a brand-new Honda CRV.

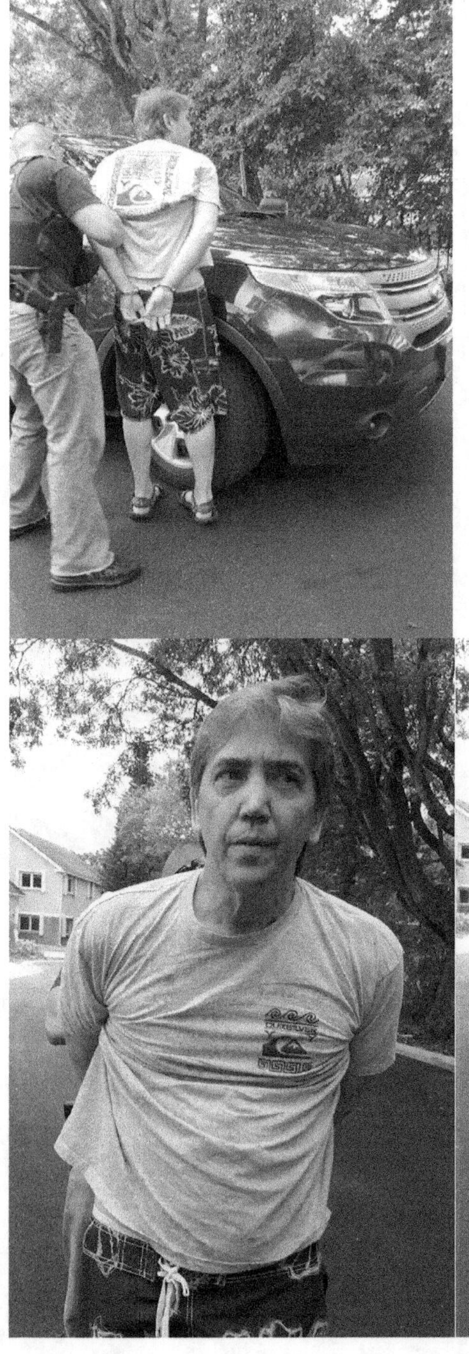

For the second time in ten months, Robert is beaten and physically abused by law enforcement officials and led away in handcuffs.

This time, the new injuries compounded the previous injuries and Robert was taken to the Broward Health Medical Center in Ft. Lauderdale, FL. for observation. He was diagnosed on August 25, 2016 with pre-cancerous bleeding polyps.

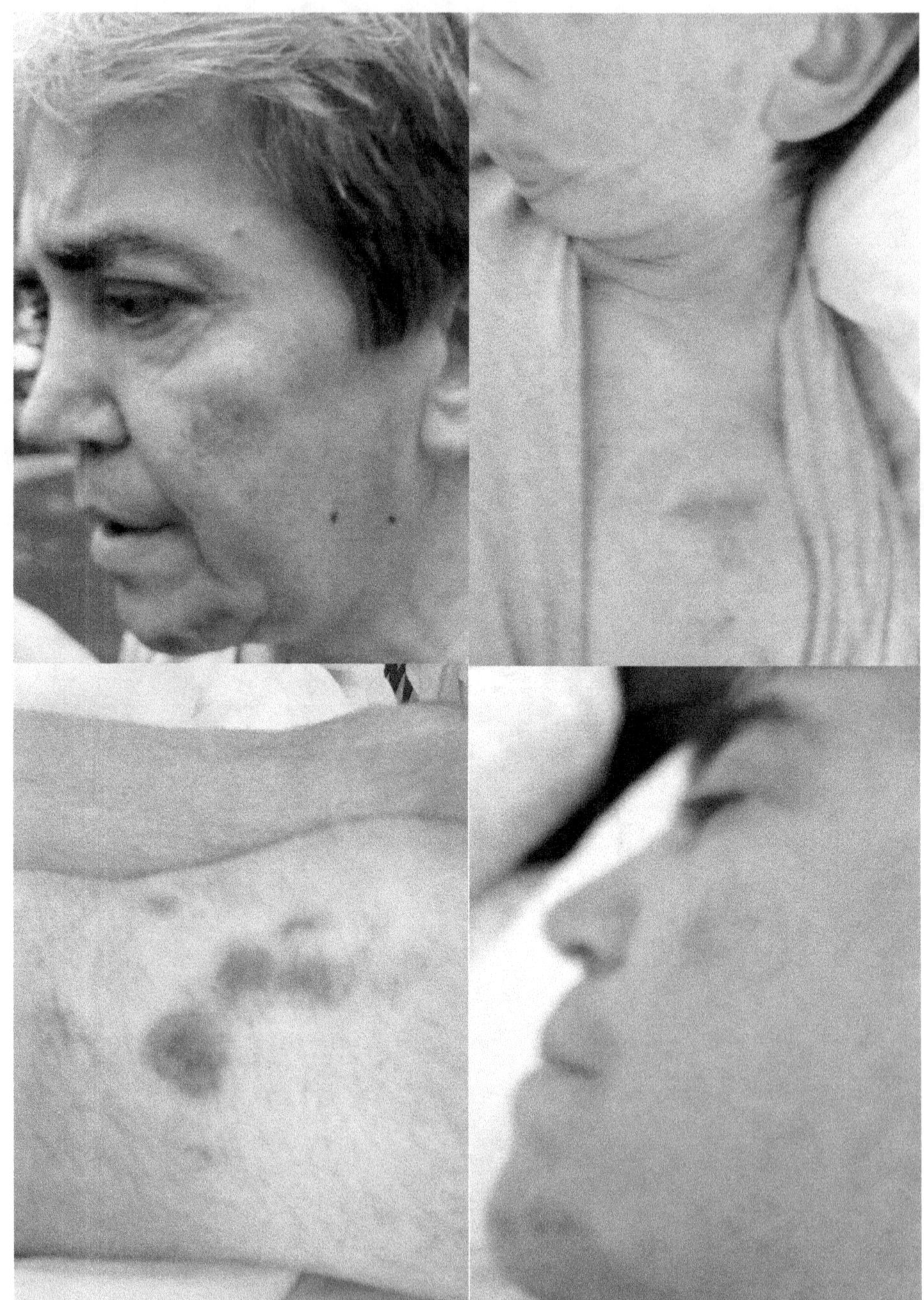

New injuries by Broward County US Marshals
add more pain for Robert!

Later I read in the police report signed by the Broward County newly hired Police Officer, who was the one whose truck smacked into our vehicle and then smashed our back window, stating: "He had to use force because Robert was running down the street." That was a lie. Robert never ran down the street. He laid face down, beside our vehicle, on the concrete road upon exiting the drivers' side, at the officer's command. I took cell phone pictures of this that were evidence against their falsifying their police report. Twice I read erroneous police reports, one in Lake County and one in Broward County. Being an eyewitness to three police officers in Broward County and three Lake County Sheriff Deputies using excessive force and erroneously stating on their police reports that my son was resisting an officer without violence, caused the prosecutor in Lake County to invalidate my son's $25,000 bond. Their bogus police report caused me to lose another $25,000 bond I paid four days earlier. More importantly, incarceration prevented Robert from receiving urgently needed medical treatment for his growing colon cancer diagnosis. Robert suffered extreme abdominal pain that only got worse over the months ahead, while the Detention Centers both denied giving him proper medical treatment for his colon cancer diagnosis that worsened into stage 4 cancer and metastasized throughout the main organs in his body.

The invalidation of this bond by the Lake County Judge led to Robert being sent back to the Lake County Detention Center, which led to my filing a civil action suit against the three police officers in Broward County. After a three-day jury trial, my son won a Not Guilty verdict, and all charges of resisting an officer were dismissed. However, the Judge in Lake County, who was biased in favor of the Lake County Deputies, ignored my son's victory verdict in Broward County and denied reinstatement of his $25,000 bond. This was largely due to the deputies falsely testifying, under oath, that my son should not be granted reinstatement of his bond because he was a danger to the community. They made up this bogus lie and told the Judge that a neighbor told them Robert and I, his seventy-nine-year-old mother, would take nightly walks in front of our gated waterfront home in Mt. Dora, Fl. They considered these mother/son nightly walks to be a danger to the community. I wasn't aware that such corruption existed among police officers to the extent that they would violate their oath of office.

During the entire seventeen years, our family lived in the Mt. Dora gated and waterfront community, as our second home, our family would often take walks together whenever weather permitted. We never once had any problems in any community we ever lived in. We were always stellar residents. The deputies lying about my son's character prevented the Judge from granting Robert his medical bond release for him to get urgently needed medical treatment for his cancer, which was rapidly growing throughout his major organs.

From August 25, 2016, Robert was denied medical treatment, hospitalization, or any proper medical care for his stage 4 colon cancer, until he almost died on April 17, 2019. The detention center rushed Robert to the hospital so he wouldn't die in his cell. He had an emergency colectomy surgery to remove his entire cancerous colon. A colostomy bag that collects fecal matter from the digestive tract was placed in the abdominal wall called a stoma. This surgical procedure severely devastated my son. The surgeon informed Robert he was terminal and didn't have long to live because cancer had spread now to all his vital organs. He said, "Mr. O'Hare if you came two days later from the detention center, you'd be dead."

Soon after this medical prognosis, Robert was released by another Judge in Lake County on a medical bond. The bogus charges, investigated by one of the three officers who assaulted Robert from Lake County, were dropped by Florida State Attorney Brad King.

The miraculous reunion of Robert and me after his incarceration of 1011 days was truly a blessing from God!

Unfortunately, our joy over his freedom was short-lived. Robert's cancer invaded his other vital organs during the next fourteen months of his life and caused him to be in acute pain every waking moment. Living without his colon and using a colostomy bag to empty his fecal matter was very gut-wrenching for him. The cancer spread to his prostate and he couldn't urinate without a catheter. Then he had to endure three successive emergency surgeries for bowel obstructions. His intestinal problems started right after his first brutal beating on October 5, 2015, by the three Lake County Sheriff Deputies, and his intestinal problems were exacerbated on August 25, 2017, when three U.S. Marshals also used physical force on Robert, when they charged Robert with phony charges of resisting an officer.

I witnessed both these two brutal police assaults on my son. I fought tirelessly to get the court system and the detention centers to give Robert urgently needed medical treatment for his colon cancer that was rapidly growing and spreading throughout his vital organs for the entire 1011 days he was incarcerated.

Robert was coming near to his last battle for life when I placed him under hospice home care for the last days of his life. On July 27, 2020, at 8:40 pm, my son passed away in agony and excruciating pain from stage 4 colon cancer. I was by his bedside holding him while two of his best friends, for over 30 years, were on each side of his hospital bed, holding his hands. The hospice nurse said the last thing to go was Robert's hearing. I used those precious moments left in Robert's life to tell him how much I loved him and what a joy he brought to me, our family, and his friends, and how proud I was of the good life he lived. I thanked him for being the best son I could ever have. During his final earthly   moments,
I felt the presence of Jesus standing by his bedside, waiting to

take him home.

The night before Robert's passing, the hospice nurse told me Robert had said the sinner's prayer. I asked, "What did he say?"

She said, your son prayed, ***"Dear Jesus, I accept you as my Savior. I love you."*** Even though our family prayed the sinner's prayer many times, his last words spoken before he went home to be with our Lord and Savior, Jesus Christ was heartwarming for me to hear. Robert's earthly body and all the pain that was in it are gone forever. In its place is a spirit-filled life with unending joy, peace, and heavenly bliss while being reunited with his sisters, Anne Marie and Patty Lynne. Soon, the Second Coming of Jesus Christ will bring all believers home to live in God's glorious kingdom and be reunited with all their saved loved ones.

My son was an innocent victim of the injustice in our legal and court system. While in the detention centers, awaiting court dates, Robert was denied his civil, constitutional, and prisoner's rights. Due to the fact I appealed his bogus charges, Robert never went to Prison and never had a jury trial in a Court of Law.

The three Lake County Sheriff Deputies and the three Broward County U.S. Marshals who violated Federal Statutes 42 U.S. Code § 1983 in using brutal police force on my son, lying on their police reports, and falsely testifying in a court of law were shielded by the law with immunity. The results of their inhuman treatment of my son and their violation of state and federal laws caused my son to endure unjust persecution that ultimately led to his death.

WARNING!

THE FOLLOWING TWO PAGES
CONTAIN DISTURBING IMAGES OF
THE RESULTS OF EXTREME POLICE
BRUTALITY AND CORRUPTION.

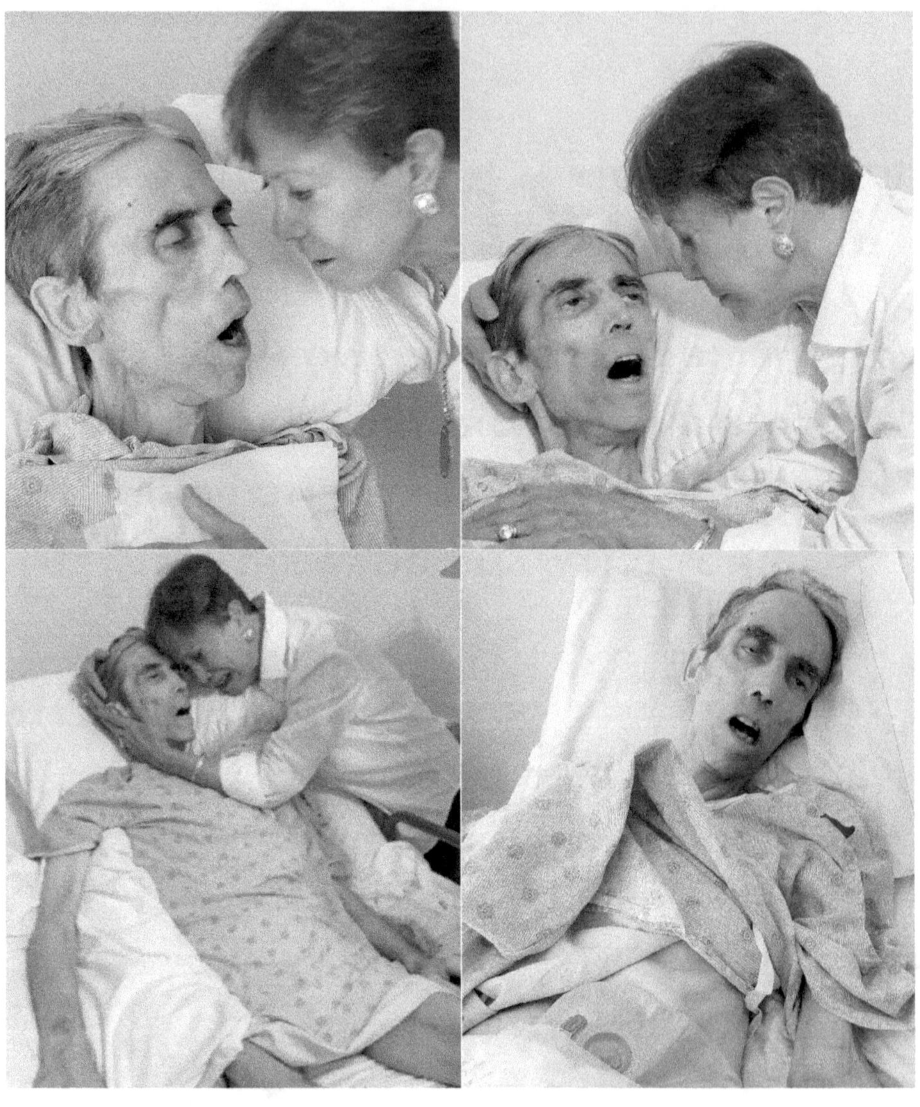

Robert Anthony O'Hare spends his final breaths with his mother, Virginia O'Hare who told him how much she loved him and how proud she was of the life he lived, and what a wonderful son he was to her. As he was gasping for his final breath, she said, "Robert, Jesus is here to take you home to be reunited with your sisters."

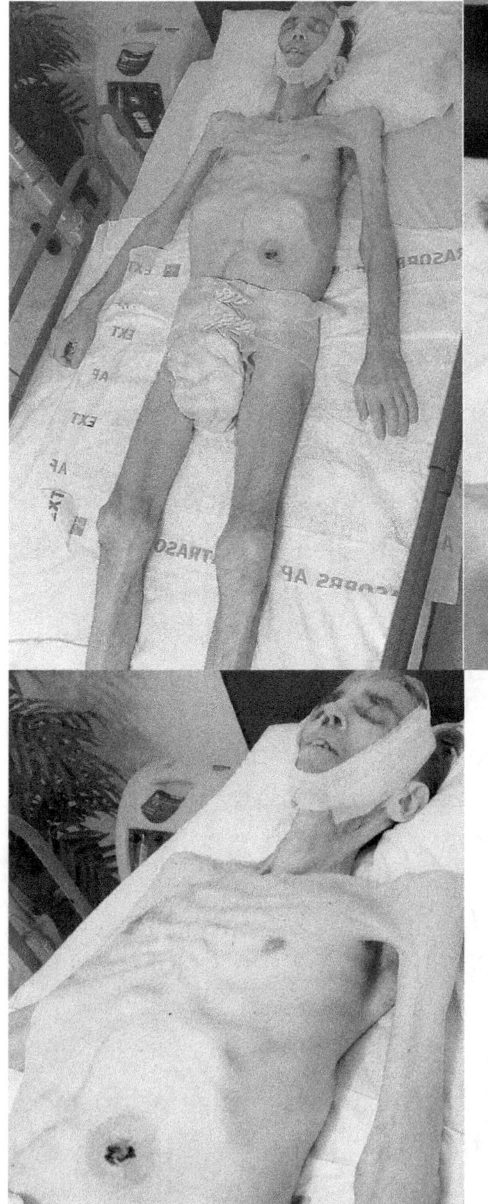

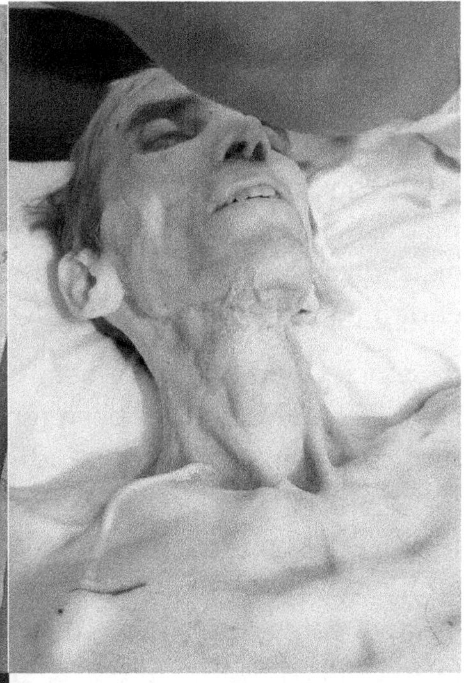

Rest in Peace, Robert! Your pain and struggle for justice are finally over. You are enjoying the awesome beauty that God has prepared for you in Heaven. Reunited with your family that passed before you, you will spend eternity with your Lord and Savior, Jesus Christ!

In Summary

Sheriff Deputies in Lake County Florida used bogus charges, lies, and corruption to cause my son, Robert Anthony O'Hare, to be unjustly incarcerated for 1011 days without being given his civil, constitutional, and prisoner's rights for urgently needed medical care and treatment for his stage 4 colon cancer. This caused cancer to metastasize throughout his vital organs which ended his life!

Since George Floyd was murdered by a Police Officer, their shield of immunity has been replaced now with JUSTICE! Currently, I have an appeal pending for a retrial in Federal Court against the three Sheriff Deputies in Lake County, Florida, for their violation of Federal Law section 1983. Evidence presented at the retrial will include the deputies lying in concert in a court of law against my son to cover over their own violations, filing false police reports, making false charges and false statements that caused every motion for Robert's medical bond to be denied, so he could not receive outside medical treatment for his colon cancer. It wasn't until Robert became terminally ill and underwent emergency surgery to remove his entire colon and was given only days to live that my motion for a Medical Bond was granted by another sitting Judge in Lake County, Florida. He granted Robert a medical bond, without the three Sheriff's Deputies being present to object.

Our civil rights laws demand the following police protocol:

A police or sheriff's department is required to protect and serve its citizens, not put them in danger, injure them or engage in offensive behavior. To protect the innocent and the vulnerable citizens, police or sheriff's departments must have rules, policies, and systems in place to ensure their employees have the proper training and tools to make encounters with citizens as safe as possible for themselves, the citizens they encounter, and all innocent bystanders.

When police officers hurt or kill the very people they are sworn to serve and protect, the law must demand accountability and sanctions against the offending officer, not grant them the shield of immunity. Our civil rights law focuses on protecting an American's Constitutional rights as guaranteed by the Bill of Rights and the Thirteenth and Fourteenth Amendments to the United States Constitution. This protects every American's rights to due process, equal treatment under the law for all people regarding enjoyment of life, liberty, property, and protection.

The three Sheriff's Deputies and the three U.S. Marshals violated state and federal laws against my son. They imposed upon him police brutality, wrongful conviction with cruel and unusual treatment. These offending officers will not find immunity from the highest Judge in the world, our almighty and omnipotent God and His Son, Jesus Christ!

"Do not take revenge, my dear friends, but leave room for God's wrath, for it is written: 'It is mine to avenge; I will repay,' says the Lord" (Romans 12:19 NIV).

I pray for justice for Robert and place all things in God's hands where vengeance and judgment belong only to Him.

Satan rules all the kingdoms of this world and uses his power to destroy the human race by pouring sin, crime, corruption, and injustice into everyone's life. His wrath against humanity has intensified because he knows his days are numbered. He is escalating his evil demonic powers throughout the entire world, causing crime to escalate and lawlessness to overflow into our Judicial system, where everyone goes to seek justice.

God's laws and man's laws are based on a judicial system., which is what our Country's laws are based on. Every citizen wants their constitutional rights upheld by our justice system, which is based on a common law system. This means that judges base their decisions on previous court rulings in similar cases, making previous decisions by a higher court binding and becoming part of the law. It is essential and very challenging for every lawyer, who represents their clients in a court of law, to keep abreast of common or case laws, which are constantly merging in Supreme Court decisions as laws. They must do so to successfully prevail in a court of law for their client's rights. The law uses these case laws to resolve ambiguities in deciding current cases. In other words, the law analyzes these former cases to resolve decisions in current cases. Using these past decisions, called case laws, are based solely on judicial decisions rather than law based on Constitutions, Statutes, or Regulations. Case law of prior decisions sets a precedent for future verdicts. Case laws are essential in our court system and are challenging to keep up with, as new ones are always added.

All decisions made by the U.S. Circuit Court of Appeals and the U.S. Supreme Court must be followed by the Federal Trials Courts. This is called following precedent. One significant case law change that was finally cast in stone by the Supreme Court came from a recent court settlement on the murder of George Floyd by a police officer. This case law emphatically states that police officers who violate Federal Statute Title 42 of United States Code Section 1983 can not use qualified immunity as their defense. They can now be found guilty and not hide behind their former defense of immunity. This is a milestone leap for justice and every victim of police abuse. My deceased son, Robert O'Hare, was a victim of being brutally beaten by three deputy sheriffs in Lake County, FL. Qualified immunity saved those deputies who violated his Fourth Amendment rights and Federal Law Section 1983. This travesty of justice was covered in my best-selling book, *Virginia O'Hare Documents God's Law Vs. Man's Law.*

Countless people who read my first book, *Virginia O'Hare's Trials, Triumphs, and Vision from God,* wanted the story to go on after they reached the last page. Barnes & Noble features this book as the best book to read for 2020. My second book, *Virginia O'Hare Documents God's Law Vs. Man's Law,* is featured by Amazon as "YOUR NEXT GREAT READ!" My third book, *Virginia O'Hare Declares God's Final Warning to the World,* was featured by Kindle Unlimited. Countless other major book marketing companies are featuring my three God-inspired prophetic books as best-selling books across the globe.

Robert Anthony and I were planning a Worldwide Ministry to fulfill my calling by God 43 years ago as His Last Day Prophet. On February 9th, 2022, the Department of the Treasury, Internal Revenue Service, determined that Virginia O'Hare World-Wide Ministry Corp under code (IRC) Section 501(C) (3) was approved as a not-for-profit private foundation. I pray the world will partner with me in my quest to seek justice for all, and to lead all souls into God's Kingdom through our Lord and Savior, Jesus Christ.

My Life in Pictures

A First Generation American

Worldwide, best-selling author Virginia O'Hare (born Virginia Pecchio) is a First Generation American. Her parents, pictured here at their wedding, John (25) and Lucy (18), were born and raised in Italy. John lived in Rome and his bride was from Florence, Italy. As a First Generation American, Virginia's story has been one that encompasses the True American Dream. From starting her own successful business with nothing more than guts and determination, to always following God's will and living with the Mantle as His chosen Last Day Prophet.

The Importance of Family

From the time she was born, Virginia learned the importance of a close-knit family. Shown here at age eleven, Virginia (second from the left) served as the Flower Girl at her older sister Mary's wedding in her hometown of Poughkeepsie, NY.

God-Given Talent

During her High School years, Virginia, an honor student, excelled with many God-given talents, earning her numerous awards and recognition. She was a frequent lead singer and performer in school plays, pageants, and musicals, and the Lead Soprano in the school's Glee Club and Church Choir. She was also a Varsity Cheerleader, and even dabbled in fashion modeling.

(see additional pictures on the next two pages)

APRIL 24, 1955. — ELMIRA

EFA Pupils To Give Program

At a meeting of the Thursday Morning Musicales April 28 at 10:15 a. m. in Beecher Hall, Park Church, a program arranged by George Abbott, supervisor of music in Elmira schools, will be presented.

The Girls Glee Club of the Elmira Free Academy will sing. Instrumental solos will be played by Elaine Grunwald, French horn, and by Nancy Keeler, oboe.

Virginia Pecchio will sing a soprano solo and Lucille Sekella and Nancy Loop will sing a duet.

The Glee Club is directed by Miss Joanne Vaisey, music instructor at EFA, and accompanist will be Jane Carlson and Diane Butters.

The girls appearing in solo or duet are specializing in study of music. Miss Grunwald, junior, plays both horn is a member of the band and orchestra, and Elmira Symphony Orc. sings in the Academy Glee chorus and octet; plans to major in music at Syracuse University.

Miss Keeler, a senior, plays oboe, clarinet and piano; has studied piano at the Eastman School of Music; has been a member of the Perry Community Chorus, and its accompanist; is a member of the Academy band, orchestra, chorus and octet; has performed in state and county

GEORGE ABBOTT, supervisor of music in Elmira schools, has arranged a program for the Thursday Morning Musicales April 28 at The Park Church. He is shown above with Miss Joanne Vaisey, left, music instructor at the Elmira Free Academy, and students Lucille Sekella, Virginia Pecchio and Nancy Loop.

GRAND FINALE. The entire cast of the third annual
lent show of the Elmira Free Academy join in singing "There's No Business Like Show Business", to
ring down the curtain.

Elmira Free Academy

Talent Show Scores Hit at EFA

**By CLARE REIDY
and BOB TATELBAUM**

The scene: a sidewalk cafe in Paris! Voila! This was the setting of the third annual Student Council talent show, held Thursday and Friday in the EFA auditorium. Academy students enjoyed every minute of the lively, fast-moving show, from the opening number by Dean Arnold's jazz band to the grand finale, a rendition of "There's No Business Like Show Business" by the entire cast.

Master of ceremonies was Marion Pirozzola, president of the Student Council. In the musical department, the following Academyites starred: Maggie Paskow, Carol Riss, George Spriggs, Carolyn Ostrander, Robert McElligott, Virginia Pecchio, Barbara Brinthaupt, Mary Bosco, and that well-known singing "combo", the Three G's (Sue Grubb, Ardith Gunderman and Magie Grant).

Dancing their way into the spotlight were: Carol Dolinsky and Gerri Rugur. Ellie Coddington and Janet Graham exhibited their skills in twirling. Chuck Sciorra, with an accordion solo, and Herb Tinney, with "The Warsaw Concerto" rounded out the show. The final number, and the one which put every member of the audience on the edge of his seat (and we don't mean figuratively) was an acrobatic dance by Dwana Lee, a "real pro."

Credit goes to George Lavris, set designer; to Teresa Di Santo, student director; and to Charles Miller, faculty adviser.

Walk-on parts were handled by Larry Keagle, Bernice Freeman, Chuck Ponzi, Bill Contando and Joe Stachowski.

* * *

MASQUERS, EFA's dramatic society, has decided on its annual play. Their choice is "Lavender and Old Lace," an old-fashioned melodrama. Tryouts will be held in the near future.

Los Diablitos, the EFA Spanish Club, will meet Tuesday, March 15, at the home of Gail Griffis. Jane Callahan, program chairman, will provide the entertainment.

—ELMIRA STAR-GAZETTE—

WIN MODELING HONORS—A party last night at the Harry B. Bentley Post American Legion Home on Lake St. ended the course for the summer of the Mil-Dor Modeling School. Awarded trophies for conscientious work were, at left: Miss Virginia Pecchio, Miss Sylvia Travis, Miss Kathy Kunth and Miss Mary Lou Personius.

(Above) Virginia was often a featured soloist at her church. The same Catholic Church that she was baptized in, received her First Communion and Confirmation, the same church she was eventually married in.

(Right) Married at age twenty to Robert O'Hare, Virginia's marriage lasted thirteen years, ending in divorce. The Catholic Church later annulled the marriage.

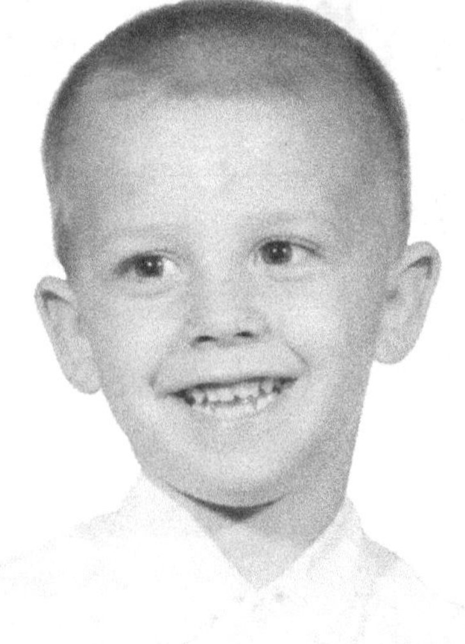

Family Time

Virginia's three children, Anne Marie *(top left)* Patricia Lynne *(top right)* and Robert Anthony *(right)* were all born within three and a half years.

Mrs. Virginia O'Hare, head of the O'Hare Personnel Agency, interviews a job applicant.

A Head for Business

Ready to make her mark on the world, Virginia became a strong entrepreneur and founded the O'Hare Personnel Agency. Her Agency soon became the Number One Personnel Agency in the Poughkeepsie, NY, area. The NY State Supervisor informed her that out of 25 offices, she makes more placements than all the other offices put together.

A Top Executive

As a top female executive, Virginia became a part of numerous trade and sales organizations as she helped lift many other young women to top management positions throughout the area.

Fame from Misfortune

Virginia won a landmark malpractice case before the New York Supreme Court against a world-famous plastic surgeon and gained global notoriety. Then at age 42, Virginia sold her home in Poughkeepsie, NY, and her successful employment agency, and moved her family to Fort Lauderdale, FL, to start a new life. You can read all the fascinating details of this story in Virginia's first book, *"Virginia O'Hare's Trials, Triumphs, and Vision from God."*

Virginia O'Hare has been living in Fort Lauderdale since her famed 1979 malpractice suit over a tummy-tuck operation.

Staff photo by DEBORAH MEEKS

Virginia O'Hare

A botched bellybutton leads to a book for the Lord

By Nora Frenkiel
Staff Writer

In January of 1979, I received a vision of a large TV screen in which I was on the screen and there were newspapers flashing in front of me from all over the country and my picture was on the front page.

Virginia O'Hare is speaking with a strange mixture of detachment and child's wonder. While listening to her, you focus on her eyes — eyes that seem to blink of their own accord.

You focus on the surroundings: the Northeast Fort Lauderdale canal-side home with plastic covers on the dining room chairs, the home that is as immaculately kept as the woman herself. The 45-year-old face is unmarred by wrinkles. She is slender and petite, and favors pastel blouses and slim skirts.

It has been three years since Miss O'Hare's vision came true.

In May 1979, she became an instant celebrity after a jury awarded her $854,219 in a malpractice suit against Dr. Howard Bellin, a prominent New York plastic surgeon. Ms. O'Hare claimed Bellin misplaced her bellybut-

> **I am writing a book that is divinely directed to give people a true picture of what it's like to undergo this trauma, this horrendous experience. I know it will be beneficial to people.**

ton during a tummy-tuck operation in 1974.

"I could go into a subway in New York and I could see my picture on the cover of the *Post*. It was a real strange feeling. What I wanted to do, since I was from a small town (Poughkeepsie, N.Y.), was scream, 'They got my picture.' "

She was a willing co-conspirator in the exploitation, the sensationalism that splashed her face and body across front pages and made her the curiosity of the week in *People* magazine. She talked willingly to anyone who asked about the horror.

More than eight years have passed since her surgery and Ms. O'Hare, who was viewed as both victim and opportunist, finally fled the spotlight for seclusion and anonymity in Fort

Lauderdale after the verdict. Yet she seems anxious to thrust herself back into its cruel glare.

Why would she subject herself to exposure again? Her answers go roundabout and settle at the beginning: the botched surgery.

"I feel very strongly that an injustice was done to my body," she says in a cool, detached voice. "What I went through when they did the unveiling was the worst moment of my life."

She sees herself as a symbol for all victims.

"I get very upset when I see people being taken advantage of, exploited, hurt, maliciously persecuted."

She leads you to the den, where there is a small bookcase crammed with medical textbooks on plastic surgery and

scrapbooks of the publicity surrounding her case.

She displays the gruesome, intimate shots that recorded "the worst moment of my life."

"Look at this," she says of a particularly ugly snapshot of an abdomen scarred and bruised, "and your hands reach out to touch what your eyes do not wish to see."

The issue of surgery remains an open wound. "I was butchered and the most important award I got was knowing I got justice in the courts. It wasn't something you get over, because somebody gives you a few thousand dollars. The money, quite honestly, was mostly given up by me."

Because the surgeon's insurance company was bankrupt, the case went to New York State's insurance commissioner who reached an agreement with Ms. O'Hare. She settled for $200,000 and moved her family to Fort Lauderdale.

"The Lord directed me here," she says.

Please see O'HARE, 5D

God's Plans for the Future

In Fort Lauderdale, she went to real estate school. She got her Florida real estate license and successfully developed a career, listing and selling multi-million-dollar waterfront properties in upscale communities. From her first year and each year after that, she maintained a #1 top producer status, which allowed her to independently support her three children and grow her real estate business into earnings of multi-millions of dollars.

An Encounter

Shortly after starting her new career in Real Estate, Virginia purchased a waterfront home on a scenic point lot in an upscale community in Fort Lauderdale, Fl. for her family, which was next to a bridge. This is where she had God's audible and visual apparition while standing alone one evening on the this bridge next to her point lot residence in Fort Lauderdale, FL.

Family is Everything

Virginia always enjoyed the blessings of a close family bond.
Meals together and holidays were particularly special to her.

Once in a Lifetime...

In 1995, Virginia took her family on a once-in-a-lifetime trip to Israel and the Holy Land, where they were all baptized in the Jordon River, where our Lord and Savior Jesus Christ was baptized by John the Baptist 2000 years ago.

JUNGLE QUEEN
kamauga Battlefield
or Center

Forever a Family Bond

Virginia and her second husband, Dan, spent 45 wonderful years together with Anne Marie, Patty Lynne, and Robert Anthony.

Their life together as a family was filled with loving, caring, and fun-filled memories. On September 30, 2013, Dan joined Anne Marie, who passed away a year earlier on September 17, 2012, and Patty Lynne joined them on November 24, 2013. Seven years later, Robert Anthony joined them on July 27, 2020.